Better
COOKING
A year in the kitchen

Published by Murdoch Books® a division of Murdoch Magazines Pty Ltd.

Published by:

Murdoch Books® Australia
GPO Box 1203
Sydney NSW 2001
Phone: +61 (0) 2 4352 7000
Fax: +61 (0) 2 4352 7026

Murdoch Books® UK
Ferry House, 51–57 Lacy Road
Putney, London SW15 1PR
Phone: +44 (0) 208 355 1480
Fax: +44 (0) 208 355 1499

Food Editor: Kerrie Carr
Editorial Director: Diana Hill
Editor: Zoë Harpham
Creative Director: Marylouise Brammer
Concept and design: Alex Frampton
Photographers: Jon Bader, Steve Brown, Louise Lister, Mark O'Meara
Stylists: Janelle Bloom, Yael Grinham, Amber Keller, Michelle Noerianto
Food consultant: Dixie Elliott
Production: Fiona Byrne

Chief Executive: Juliet Rogers
Publisher: Kay Scarlett

National Library of Australia Cataloguing-in-Publication Data:
Carr, Kerrie. Better cooking: a year in the kitchen
Includes index. ISBN 174045 253 4
1. Cookery. I.Title II. Title: Better homes and gardens
641.564

We have used 20 ml tablespoon measures. If you are using a 15 ml tablespoon, for most
recipes the difference will not be noticeable. However, for recipes using small amounts of flour
and cornflour, add an extra teaspoon for each tablespoon specified.

IMPORTANT: Those who might be at risk from the effects of salmonella poisoning (the elderly,
pregnant women, young children and those suffering from immune deficiency diseases)
should consult their GP with any concerns about eating raw eggs.

Better
COOKING
A year in the kitchen

Kerrie Carr

MURDOCH
BOOKS

Contents

Spring

Summer

Autumn

Winter

Foreword

There is nothing in life more important than food and eating. Indeed, apart from simply keeping us alive, it also gives us the opportunity to nurture those we love, entertain those whose company we enjoy and impress anyone we choose at anytime! And, of course, the activity of cooking itself is very therapeutic. For my part, I believe there is nothing more seductive and satisfying than feeding people well.

It has long been the philosophy of Better Homes and Gardens® to provide recipes that are delicious and simple to prepare, but that also incorporate new ingredients, techniques and culinary skills we all deserve to know. This collection of recipes, from the heart and soul of Food Editor Kerrie Carr, encapsulates all that is truly remarkable about cooking and includes a plethora of delicious dishes that you'll love to cook. Own this book and you can live from it forever.

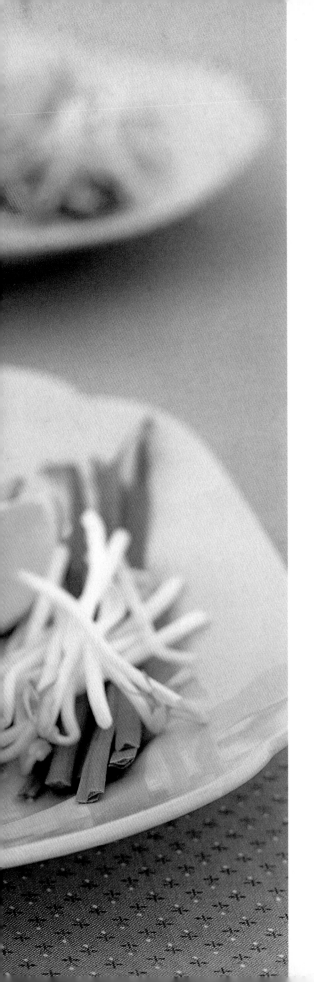

Spring

All about
herbs

Fresh herbs are fabulously sensuous.
Not only do they taste great, they're also
beautiful to look at, wonderful to touch
and tantalizing to smell. There are dozens
of culinary herbs and each has its own
special attributes that can add a subtle (or
not so subtle) difference to your cooking.

Growing herbs

If you have herbs growing in pots or
a patch, it's so simple and satisfying to
be able to pick off just what you want.
Nurseries generally stock a large range
of herb seedlings so it's easy to start
growing them yourself.

Put your favourite herbs in pots and
keep them on the kitchen windowsill,
ripe for the picking. Parsley, rosemary,
sage, thyme and coriander (cilantro) are
a good start, then you can experiment
with others – whatever you're cooking,
you're sure to find a herb that will turn
an everyday dish into something special.

Kitchen combos

There are some herb packs available that make starting
your own herb garden easy. You'll find Mediterranean,
Asian and Kitchen combinations; pick the ones that suit
the type of cooking you do the most. Sit them on the
kitchen bench and pick what you need or plant them in
pots or the garden. Look for them in your local nursery.
It's also easy to make your own combinations by picking
herbs from a particular region and planting them together.

Buying and storing herbs

Whether you're buying them in cut bunches or as seedlings to grow, choose herbs that look fresh. They should be a good colour, have firm stems and no brown leaves or marks.

You can buy bunches of herbs from most supermarkets and greengrocers. Keep the bunch at its best by placing it in a jug of fresh water. Cover with a plastic bag and store in the fridge, changing the water daily. Herbs can also be wrapped in damp paper towels or a clean tea towel, covered with plastic wrap and stored in the vegetable crisper in the fridge.

Crush a few fresh herbs with your fingers then breathe in their wonderful aroma.

Gnocchi with sage and burnt butter sauce

Preparation time:

20 mins

Cooking time:

20 mins

SERVES 4

1 kg (2 lb 4 oz) desiree potatoes

2 tablespoons olive oil

1/2 teaspoon sea salt

1/2 teaspoon white pepper

250 g (2 cups) plain (all-purpose) flour

90 g (3 1/4 oz) butter

12–16 sage leaves

2 cloves garlic, cut into slivers

flaked pecorino cheese, for serving, optional

1 Wash the potatoes well, then place in a large pan, cover with cold water, put the lid on and bring to the boil. Simmer until very tender. Drain, set aside to cool, but do not rinse. When cool enough to handle, gently peel and discard the skin.

2 Put the potatoes in a large bowl and mash. Mix in the olive oil, salt and pepper. Add the flour and mix until just combined. Place the mixture on a lightly floured surface and gently knead until it forms a smooth ball.

3 Divide the mixture into four pieces. Knead each piece into a ball, then roll each out to form a sausage shape about 2.5 cm (1 inch) thick. Cut each sausage shape into pieces about 4 cm (1 1/2 inches) long. Roll each piece of dough (now gnocchi) on the inside of a fork to form ridges. Place on a lightly floured tea towel.

4 Bring a large pan of water to the boil. Add the gnocchi a few at a time. Cook for 3–4 minutes or until they rise to the surface and float. Remove with a slotted spoon, place in a well-greased ovenproof dish and keep warm in a low oven. Continue cooking in this way until all the gnocchi have been cooked.

5 Just before serving, heat the butter in a small heavy-based pan until it starts to foam. Add the sage and garlic and cook until the butter turns nut brown. Remove from the heat and immediately pour over the gnocchi. Top with flaked pecorino cheese, if desired.

Lebanese bread salad

Preparation time:

20 mins

Cooking time:

5 mins

SERVES 4

vegetable oil

2 rounds Lebanese bread

3 Lebanese (short) cucumbers, finely chopped

5 tomatoes, finely chopped

1 bunch radishes, finely chopped

1 red capsicum (pepper), finely chopped

1 green capsicum (pepper), finely chopped

5 spring onions (scallions), thinly sliced

2 teaspoons paprika or sumac (from speciality
   spice shops)

40 g (½ bunch) mint, finely chopped

50 g (½ bunch) flat-leaf (Italian) parsley, finely chopped

juice of 2 lemons

60 ml (¼ cup) olive oil

salt and freshly ground black pepper

1   Pour in enough oil to fill one-third of a medium-sized, heavy-based pan and
    heat until a cube of bread dropped into the oil sizzles. Tear the Lebanese
    bread into large pieces and deep-fry in batches until golden brown. Drain
    on paper towel.

2   Put the cucumbers, tomatoes, radishes, capsicums, spring onions, paprika,
    mint and parsley in a serving bowl.

3   Whisk the lemon juice, olive oil, salt and pepper in a small bowl. Pour over the
    vegetables and toss well. Place the bread on a serving platter and top with the
    dressed salad. Serve immediately.

Fish with potato and thyme

Preparation time:

20 mins

Cooking time:

25 mins

SERVES 4

5 medium-sized purple congo potatoes (see Cook's tips)

750 g (1 lb 10 oz) deep-sea perch (also known as
ocean perch or coral perch), cut into 14 cm (5½ inch)
long pieces (see Cook's tips)

3 zucchini (courgettes)

juice of 1 lemon, plus wedges for serving

sea salt flakes

freshly ground black pepper

10 g (½ bunch) sprigs thyme

2 slices bread

20 g (¾ oz) butter

1 tablespoon olive oil

2 cloves garlic, finely chopped

1. Preheat the oven to 200°C (400°F/Gas 6). Place four sheets of baking paper onto a flat workbench. Wash the potatoes and then slice very thinly. Place slices of potato, overlapping slightly, in two rows down the centre of each sheet of baking paper. Arrange the fish pieces on top of the potatoes.

2. Using a vegetable peeler, slice thin ribbons down the length of the zucchini, then pile the ribbons on top of the fish. Sprinkle lemon juice, salt and pepper over the zucchini, then add sprigs of thyme on top. Wrap the baking paper around the food, making four secure parcels. Put the parcels on a baking tray and bake for 20–25 minutes or until the fish is cooked through.

3. Put the bread in the bowl of a small food processor and process until breadcrumbs form. Melt the butter with the oil in a large non-stick frypan. Add the breadcrumbs and garlic, then cook over a medium heat, stirring occasionally, until golden brown.

4. Serve the fish topped with the garlic and breadcrumb mixture with a lemon wedge on the side.

Crispy chicken with coriander pesto

Preparation time:

15 mins

Cooking time:

25 mins

SERVES 4

2 cloves garlic

1 teaspoon sea salt flakes

90 g (1 bunch) coriander (cilantro), leaves and roots only

115 g (3/4 cup) blanched whole almonds

1–2 small red chillies

100 ml (3 1/2 fl oz) olive oil

4 chicken breasts, on the bone, with skin

4 red capsicums (peppers)

a little olive oil

sea salt flakes

freshly ground black pepper

1   Preheat the oven to 200°C (400°F/Gas 6). Place the garlic, salt, coriander, almonds and chillies into the bowl of a food processor. Process until a thick paste forms. With the food processor running, slowly add the oil. Continue to process until a smooth, bright green paste or pesto forms. Scoop into a bowl.

2   Place the chicken breasts on a flat surface. Using your fingers, gently lift the skin away from the flesh, forming a pocket. Spoon some pesto under the skin and spread evenly over the flesh. Put the chicken into a shallow ovenproof dish and bake for 20–25 minutes or until the skin is golden brown and crisp and the chicken is cooked through. Serve the chicken with roasted capsicums.

3   To roast the capsicums cut them into quarters lengthways and remove the seeds. Place the pieces on a baking tray lined with baking paper and drizzle with olive oil. Sprinkle with sea salt flakes and freshly ground black pepper. Roast until tender.

Spaghetti with rosemary and prosciutto

Preparation time:

20 mins

Cooking time:

15 mins

SERVES 4

500 g (1 lb 2 oz) spaghetti

salt

10 slices prosciutto

40 g (1½ oz) butter

2 tablespoons olive oil

400 g (14 oz) button mushrooms, sliced

extra 30 g (1 oz) butter

juice and thinly sliced zest of 1 orange

125 ml (½ cup) white wine

leaves from 4 sprigs of fresh rosemary

freshly ground black pepper

1 Cook the spaghetti in a large pan of salted boiling water for 8–10 minutes or until just tender. Drain, leaving a little water clinging to the pasta. Return to the pan and keep warm.

2 Put the prosciutto slices into a large, hot, non-stick frypan. Cook for 3–4 minutes, then turn and cook for a further 1–2 minutes or until crisp. Remove and allow to cool. When cool enough to touch, break into shards.

3 Melt half the butter with half the oil in the same frypan. Add half the mushrooms and cook over a medium heat until golden brown on both sides. Remove from the pan. Add the remaining butter and oil to the pan and cook the remaining mushrooms in the same way.

4 Melt the extra butter in a pan. Stir in the orange zest strips, orange juice, wine and rosemary. Bring to the boil, then simmer until the sauce thickens slightly and is reduced by one-third.

5 Add the prosciutto pieces, mushrooms and rosemary sauce to the pasta. Season with black pepper and toss to combine. Serve immediately.

All about
noodles

Have you ever stood flummoxed in the noodle aisle of the supermarket wondering what noodles are what and how to cook them? The huge range of fresh, dried and vacuum-packed Asian noodles now available can be confusing. So here's a guide to four of the most popular styles to start you on your way to noodle know-how.

Slurp those noodles

In Asian countries people eat noodles by sucking them up as noisily as possible. There are two reasons for this. Soup stocks are always served very hot. Slurping the noodles in the soup adds air and helps to cool the liquid as you eat the noodles. Slurping is also said to be a sign of ultimate enjoyment of your bowl of noodles.

So, enjoy noodles oriental style...slippery, slinky and slurpy.

Soba noodles

Soba noodles (left) are widely used in Japanese cuisine. You'll find beige, brown and green varieties. They are made from a combination of wheat and buckwheat flour. They have a distinctive nutty flavour and are just as good served hot or cold. The cooking process is a little different than other noodles – you add cold water at intervals while the noodles are cooking.

What noodle is that?

Hokkien (egg) noodles are yellow and have a texture much like thick spaghetti. They are available fresh from the chilled section or in vacuum packs on the shelf. These noodles are at their best in a stir-fry, particularly ones with Chinese and Malaysian flavours.

Bean thread vermicelli (at back) are also called bean thread, cellophane, transparent or glass noodles. They are very thin, dry, brittle opaque noodles that must be soaked in boiling water before use. After soaking, the noodles become transparent and very slippery. They are perfect for soups and dishes with lots of sauce.

Rice stick noodles (on bottom) are broad rice noodles ranging from 2.5 mm (1/8 inch) to 5 mm (1/4 inch) in width. They are strong and can either be boiled for three to five minutes or covered with boiling water and left to soak for seven to 10 minutes. Soaking gives them a chewy texture while boiling gives a soft, slippery texture. See the box on page 22 for details on soba noodles.

An old Chinese adage says that eating noodles will almost certainly give you a long life full of happiness.

Pad Thai

Preparation time:

25 mins

Cooking time:

10 mins

SERVES 4

250 g (9 oz) rice stick noodles

100 g (3 1/2 oz) firm tofu, cut into cubes

2 tablespoons cornflour (cornstarch)

80 ml (1/3 cup) peanut oil

3 French shallots, thinly sliced

750 g (1 lb 10 oz) raw prawns (shrimp), peeled, deveined and chopped

2 small birdseye chillies, finely chopped

juice of 2 limes

80 ml (1/3 cup) fish sauce

1 tablespoon palm sugar (see Cook's tip)

2 eggs, lightly beaten

80 g (1/2 cup) finely chopped roasted peanuts

125 g (4 1/2 oz) bean sprouts, tails removed

75 g (1/2 bunch) garlic chives, chopped

45 g (1/2 bunch) coriander (cilantro), finely chopped

Extra, for serving

75 g (1/2 bunch) garlic chives

80 g (1/2 cup) finely chopped roasted peanuts

2 limes, cut into wedges

chopped fresh chilli or chilli flakes

125 g (4 1/2 oz) bean sprouts, tails removed

1 Soak the noodles in warm water for 8 minutes. Drain well and rinse under cold water.

2 Toss the tofu in cornflour. Heat a wok over a high heat until hot. Add 60 ml (1/4 cup) of the oil, heat for 1 minute longer, then add the tofu and cook for 1–2 minutes or until golden. Remove the tofu with a slotted spoon to a plate lined with paper towel. Discard the oil in the wok. Pour the remaining oil into the wok. Add the shallots and cook over a medium to high heat, stirring until well browned. Remove and set aside.

3 Add the prawns and chillies to the wok and stir for 1–2 minutes or until the prawns turn orange. Add the noodles to the pan with the lime juice, fish sauce and palm sugar. Toss well. Add the beaten eggs and toss again. Add the tofu, peanuts, bean sprouts, chives and coriander and toss a final time to thoroughly combine. Serve with extra garlic chives, peanuts, lime wedges, chilli and bean sprouts.

Pork and noodle stir-fry

Preparation time:

10 mins plus
20 mins soaking

Cooking time:

15 mins

SERVES 4

90 g (1 cup) dried sliced Chinese mushrooms

1 tablespoon oil

375 g (1 bunch) bok choy (pak choi), trimmed

2 teaspoons sesame oil

750 g (1 lb 10 oz) pork fillets, cut into thin strips

60 g (½ cup) walnuts, roughly chopped

400 g (14 oz) Hokkien (egg) noodles

125 ml (½ cup) oyster sauce

60 ml (¼ cup) dry sherry

1 tablespoon soft brown sugar

1 tablespoon soy sauce

1 Put the mushrooms in a large bowl, cover with boiling water and allow to stand for 25–30 minutes or until tender. Drain thoroughly.

2 Heat a wok over a high heat until hot, then add the oil and heat for 1 minute longer. Add the bok choy and cook for 1–2 minutes or until the bok choy becomes bright green and tender. Add the sesame oil and toss until well combined. Remove and keep warm.

3 Add half of the pork and cook for 2–3 minutes, stirring continuously until golden brown in colour. Remove from the wok. Cook the remaining meat in the same way. Return all the meat to the wok.

4 Add the mushrooms, walnuts, noodles and the oyster sauce combined with the sherry, brown sugar and soy sauce. Toss for 1–2 minutes or until the noodles have separated and are well coated in the sauce. Place the bok choy onto serving plates and top with pork and noodles.

Chilli beef with plum sauce and noodles

Preparation time:

15 mins

Cooking time:

15 mins

COOK'S TIP

Yellow plum sauce is available from most supermarkets. The difference between it and red plum sauce is primarily colour. The red sort works just as well in this recipe.

SERVES 4

200 g (7 oz) bean thread vermicelli

750 g (1 lb 10 oz) rib eye steaks (about 3 steaks)

freshly ground black pepper

sea salt flakes

1 tablespoon oil

125 g (½ bunch) spring onions (scallions), trimmed and cut into 5 cm (2 inch) pieces

2 cloves garlic, finely chopped

2 birdseye chillies, finely chopped

125 ml (½ cup) yellow plum sauce (see Cook's tip)

1 Put the noodles in a large bowl. Cover with warm water soak for about 15 minutes or until tender. Drain thoroughly.

2 Remove any excess fat and sinew from the steaks. Sprinkle generously on both sides with freshly ground black pepper and sea salt flakes. Heat the oil in a large frypan. Add the steaks and cook over a medium to high heat for 3 minutes. Turn the steaks and cook for a further 2–3 minutes. Remove the steaks, place on a plate, cover with foil and set to one side.

3 Add the spring onions to the pan and cook until bright green in colour. Remove from the pan. If required, add a tablespoon of oil to the pan. Add the garlic and chillies and cook for 1–2 minutes before adding the noodles and plum sauce. Toss continuously until heated through and well combined.

4 Using a sharp knife cut the steaks, across the grain, into thin slices. Divide the the noodles among four serving plates. Top with slices of steak and the spring onions. Serve immediately.

Chicken, ginger and cucumber salad with wasabi dressing

Preparation time:

15 mins

Cooking time:

20 mins

COOK'S TIPS

You'll find wasabi powder in Asian grocery stores and the Asian section of supermarkets. Wasabi paste can also be used. If you don't have a bamboo steamer, the chicken breasts can be cooked in a small amount of simmering water. Drain well before slicing.

SERVES 4

3 large chicken breast fillets

250 g (9 oz) soba noodles

80 ml (1/3 cup) mirin or dry sherry

60 ml (1/4 cup) teriyaki sauce

1 teaspoon sugar

1 teaspoon wasabi powder (see Cook's tips)

50 g (1 3/4 oz) pickled ginger, drained

1 Lebanese (short) cucumber, peeled and
   cut into thin strips

1 Line the base of a large bamboo steamer with baking paper. Put the chicken into the steamer. Fill a large pan with water and bring to a simmer. Position the bamboo steamer securely on top of the pan. Cover with the steamer lid and cook the chicken for 15–20 minutes or until cooked through and tender. Cover and keep warm. Just before serving, slice the chicken.

2 Half-fill a large pan with water, bring to the boil, add the soba noodles and, when the water returns to the boil, add 250 ml (1 cup) of cold water. Repeat this process two times or until the noodles are cooked but are still a little firm to the bite. Drain, rinse in cold water and set aside.

3 While the noodles are cooking, put the mirin, teriyaki sauce and sugar into a small pan. Heat, stirring continuously until the sugar dissolves. Remove from the heat and cool in the refrigerator. Add the wasabi powder and stir well.

4 Make nests of noodles on four serving plates. Top with sliced chicken, pickled ginger and cucumber. Drizzle with sauce. Serve immediately.

filo pastry

Some say filo, some say phyllo and some even say yufka (that's Turkish). But however you say or spell it, it's a wonderful pastry that's easy to use and produces layers of crisp, golden, delicate flakes that melt in the mouth. It does need to be handled with a little care, but once you know the rules, you'll be amazed at how easy it is.

Buying and storing filo

- Filo can be purchased frozen or chilled from most supermarkets and delis.
- Chilled filo stores well for up to two months in the refrigerator. Bring chilled filo to room temperature before using (allow about 40 minutes).
- Once thawed, any unused frozen filo sheets can be stored in the refrigerator for up to a month – do not refreeze them.
- Cold filo is very brittle, so defrost frozen filo in its packaging until fully thawed. Thawing takes about two hours.

Capers and anchovies

Capers and anchovies are the perfect partners. They are especially good when added to black olives to make a rich moist tapenade, as in the Tuna and tomato tarts with olive tapenade (page 34). But if you find the tapenade too strong, you can serve the tarts with pesto or sour cream instead.

Working with filo

- Count out the number of sheets you need (your recipe should specify this), then re-roll and refrigerate any remaining sheets in their original plastic wrapper.

- Cover the sheets you are about to use with a clean, dry tea towel, then cover this with a slightly wet and well wrung out tea towel. A damp cloth placed directly on the filo can cause the sheets to stick together.

- Brush the sheets of filo with melted unsalted butter, olive oil or a combination of both using light, even strokes. You'll find butter gives the best flavour for sweet foods, while olive oil works best for savoury dishes.

- A large brush can make the process of brushing filo sheets quicker and easier. An inexpensive paintbrush will work just as well as a special pastry brush.

Use this fine paper-like pastry as a wrapping for sweet and savoury delights.

Tuna and tomato tarts with olive tapenade

Preparation time:

20 mins

Cooking time:

30 mins

COOK'S TIP

Roasting the tomatoes before adding them to the tarts removes some of the moisture that could make the pastry turn soggy.

MAKES 6 TARTS

250 g (9 oz) cherry tomatoes

olive oil

sea salt flakes

6 sheets filo pastry

melted butter

3 hard-boiled eggs, sliced

425 g (15 oz) canned tuna in brine (chunky style), drained

1 small lemon, peel and pith removed, flesh thinly sliced

Tapenade

1 clove garlic

40 g (1½ oz) anchovies, drained

1 tablespoon capers

135 g (1 cup) black olives, pitted

1 tablespoon olive oil

1 tablespoon white-wine vinegar

1 Preheat the oven to 200°C (400°F/Gas 6). Line a baking tray with baking paper. Brush the tomatoes with olive oil or spray with olive oil cooking spray. Sprinkle with sea salt flakes. Bake for 10–12 minutes or until soft and the skin begins to split. Remove from the oven and allow to cool.

2 Lay a sheet of pastry on a flat workbench. Brush with melted butter, then fold it in half from the short side. Brush again and fold in half into a rectangle. Repeat with the remaining five sheets of pastry.

3 Put a few egg slices in the centre of each pastry rectangle. Top with some tuna, leaving a 3 cm (1¼ inch) border. Put a couple of lemon slices on the tuna and top with the roasted tomatoes. Fold in the longest edges towards the filling, then the short ends. The centre of each parcel should remain open. Brush or spray with oil. Lift onto the prepared baking tray. Bake for 20 minutes or until the pastry is lightly browned, crisp and cooked underneath.

4 Meanwhile, to make the tapenade, put the garlic, anchovies and capers into the bowl of a small food processor. Process for 1 minute or until finely chopped. Add the olives, oil and vinegar. Process again until a smooth paste forms. Serve the tarts with a good dollop of tapenade and a green salad.

Smoked salmon quiche

Preparation time:	**SERVES 4**
15 mins	8 sheets filo pastry
	40 g (1½ oz) butter, melted
Cooking time:	200 g (7 oz) smoked salmon, roughly chopped
35 mins	30 g (1 bunch) chives, half finely chopped, the rest left whole
	4 eggs
	300 ml (10½ fl oz) cream
	125 ml (½ cup) milk
	salt and freshly ground black pepper

1   Preheat the oven to 180°C (350°F/Gas 4). Lightly grease a 30 x 22 x 6 cm (12 x 9 x 2½ inches) ovenproof dish. Lay a sheet of filo pastry on a workbench and lightly brush with melted butter. Fold it in half from the short side. Lift into the prepared dish, covering half the base and one long side. Brush the next sheet of filo pastry with butter and fold in half as before. Lift into the dish, covering the remaining half of the base and the other long side. Continue with the remaining sheets of pastry, layering in this way.

2   Spread the salmon evenly onto the pastry base, then sprinkle with the chopped chives. Put the eggs, cream, milk, salt and pepper in a bowl and whisk until well combined. Carefully pour over the salmon and chives. Place the remaining half bunch of chives in the centre of the custard filling. Bake for 30–35 minutes or until the filling is set and golden.

Ricotta and Gruyère strudel

Preparation time:

20 mins

Cooking time:

30 mins

COOK'S TIP

Use fresh ricotta purchased
by weight from a delicatessen,
not the packet sort found in
the refrigerated dairy section
of supermarekts.

SERVES 6

2 tablespoons olive oil

80 g (1 cup) fresh white breadcrumbs

50 g (1 3/4 oz) flaked almonds

10 g (1/2 bunch) lemon thyme, leaves only

25 g (1 oz) butter

4 spring onions (scallions), chopped

500 g (1 lb 2 oz) fresh ricotta cheese (see Cook's tip)

125 g (4 1/2 oz) Gruyère cheese, grated

2 eggs, lightly beaten

40 g (1/4 cup) plain (all-purpose) flour

finely grated zest of 1 lemon

1/4 teaspoon ground mace

salt and freshly ground black pepper

8 sheets filo pastry

80 ml (1/3 cup) olive oil

1   Preheat the oven to 200°C (400°F/Gas 6). Line a baking tray with baking paper. Heat the oil in a frypan. Add the breadcrumbs and flaked almonds and cook over a medium heat, stirring, until browned. Transfer to a bowl. Add the lemon thyme and stir well. Set aside.

2   Heat the butter in the same pan. Add the spring onions and cook over a medium heat until soft, but not brown. Transfer to a bowl. Add the ricotta, Gruyère, eggs, flour, lemon zest and mace. Season to taste with salt and pepper. Mix well to combine.

3   Place a sheet of filo on a flat surface. Brush with oil, top with another sheet of filo and brush with oil again. Sprinkle evenly with a third of the breadcrumb mixture. Continue layering in this way, finishing with filo.

4   Spoon the ricotta mixture down one long side of the filo, 5 cm (2 inches) in from the edge and 5 cm (2 inches) in from each short edge. Fold in the short edges. Fold up from the long edge and roll to form a sausage shape. Lay the roll on the prepared tray with the seam underneath and then brush with oil. Make slashes on the diagonal about 3 cm (1 1/4 inches) apart down the length of the roll. Bake for 10 minutes at 200°C (400°F/Gas 6) then reduce the oven to 180°C (350°F/Gas 4) and bake for a further 15–20 minutes. Serve in slices.

Custard rolls

Preparation time:

45 mins

Cooking time:

15 mins

MAKES 30 ROLLS

375 ml (1 1/2 cups) milk

80 g (1/3 cup) caster (superfine) sugar

60 g (1/2 cup) semolina

grated zest of 1 small lemon

1 egg, lightly beaten

20 sheets filo pastry

60 g (2 1/4 oz) unsalted butter, melted

2 tablespoons sifted icing (confectioners') sugar,
   for dusting

1 To make the custard, combine the milk, caster sugar, semolina and lemon zest in a medium-sized, heavy-based pan. Stir continuously over a medium heat until the mixture comes to the boil. Simmer for 1 minute.

2 Remove the mixture from the heat and gradually whisk in the beaten egg. Pour the custard mixture into a bowl, cover with plastic wrap to prevent a skin forming and then set aside to cool. Preheat the oven to 180°C (350°F/Gas 4). Lightly grease a baking tray.

3 Working with two sheets of filo at a time, lay the pastry on a workbench. Brush the first piece with butter, then top with the second piece. Cut the sheets lengthways from the short side into three even strips. Brush the edges with melted butter.

4 Spoon about 2 teaspoons of cooled custard 5 cm (2 inches) in from the short edge of each pastry strip. Roll the pastry over the filling, fold the ends in, and roll to the end. Repeat with the remaining pastry and custard.

5 Arrange the filled rolls on the prepared tray about 2 cm (3/4 inch) apart. Brush with the remaining butter. Bake for 12–15 minutes or until the pastry is puffed and lightly golden. Place on a wire rack to cool. Dust with icing sugar.

Pack a
picnic

Spring is a beautiful time of the year to eat outside.

There is nothing better than packing up food, blankets,

chairs, bats and balls and getting out into the fresh air.

There are so many places to choose – parks, beaches,

bushland or even your own backyard. Feeding a crowd?

Use the entire picnic menu on the following pages. Or

select a few recipes for a more modest offering.

Don't have a 'proper' picnic hamper? No matter.
Any large container, like this galvanized tub,
will do. Look around the home and you'll soon
discover there are many options. Try a wicker
laundry basket, a collection of straw baskets, a
stripey canvas beach bag or even a battered old
school case. And they will only add charm to your
spread. Just be careful that you pack everything
securely so that it arrives intact.

Picnic check list

Don't leave home without:

- A cooler or chiller box for any perishable food.
- Ice – make sure ice bricks are well frozen. Loose ice should be contained in leak-proof plastic.
- Rigid lunch boxes or containers to prevent food being squashed and spoiled.
- Crockery and cutlery – plastic will do, or use your normal dinnerware – and plenty of paper or linen napkins. Pack it all in a separate box so it is easy to find.
- Little spill-proof containers of salt, pepper and your other favourite condiments, such as mustard.
- Unbreakable glasses. These are available from most supermarkets and department stores at a reasonable price.
- A corkscrew and bottle opener.
- A serrated knife for cutting bread and meat.
- A roll of paper towels or a pack of pre-moistened towelettes for sticky fingers or to clean up spills.

Pick a spot under a tree, beside the river or on the beach, then relax and enjoy the feast.

Egg and bacon pies

Preparation time:

20 mins

Cooking time:

25 mins

MAKES 10 PIES

6 rashers bacon, rind removed, thinly sliced

375 g (3 cups) plain (all-purpose) flour

2 teaspoons dry mustard

2 tablespoons poppy seeds

125 g (4 1/2 oz) butter

170 ml (2/3 cup) water

30 g (1 bunch) chives, finely chopped

10 x 59 g (2 1/4 oz) eggs

freshly ground black pepper

sea salt flakes

1 Preheat the oven to 200°C (400°F/Gas 6). Lightly grease 10 standard muffin tins. Cook the bacon in a small frypan on a low heat until it is brown and crispy.

2 Sift the flour and mustard into a bowl, add the poppy seeds and stir well. Put the butter and water in a small pan and stir over a low heat until the butter has melted, without letting the mixture boil.

3 Make a well in the centre of the dry ingredients, pour in the butter mixture and stir until the mixture is well combined. Use your hand to bring the mixture together to form a ball. Transfer to a lightly floured board and knead gently until the pastry is smooth.

4 Roll the pastry into a sausage shape, remove one-third of the pastry, wrap it in plastic wrap and set it aside. Cut the remaining two-thirds into 10 pieces. Roll into balls. Roll each ball out to a 10 cm (4 inch) round. Gently place each round into a muffin tin; the pastry should come about 1 cm (1/2 inch) above the top of the tin.

5 Using half the bacon, put a small amount in the base of each pastry case and top with a little of the chopped chives. Break an egg into each pastry cup and top with the remaining bacon and chives. Grind over some black pepper. Cut the reserved pastry into 10 even pieces and form each into a ball. Roll the balls out to fit the top of the pies. Cut a cross in the top of each round and put on top of the pies, gently pressing the edges together to seal. Brush with water and sprinkle with sea salt. Bake for 20–25 minutes or until the pastry is golden brown and crisp. Remove from the oven and leave the pies in the tin for 10 minutes. Remove the pies from tin and stand on a wire rack to cool, or serve hot.

Potato and broad bean salad

Preparation time:

20 mins

Cooking time:

15 mins

SERVES 6

1.25 kg (2 lb 12 oz) kipfler potatoes

500 g (1 lb 2 oz) packet frozen broad (fava) beans

2 sticks celery, thinly sliced

60 ml (¼ cup) red-wine vinegar

60 ml (¼ cup) virgin olive oil

1 teaspoon Dijon mustard

salt and freshly ground black pepper

1 Wash and scrub the potatoes, then cut them into 1 cm (½ inch) chunks. Put them in a heavy-based pan, cover with cold water, bring slowly to the boil and cook until just tender, then drain. Scoop them into a large bowl.

2 Put the frozen beans in a small, heavy-based pan, cover with cold water and bring slowly to the boil. Cook for 1 minute, then drain and rinse with cold water until the beans are cool enough to handle. Remove the outer skin from each bean. Add the beans to the potatoes along with the celery, then toss to combine.

3 To make the dressing, put the vinegar, oil, mustard and salt and pepper into a small bowl and whisk with a fork to combine. Pour the dressing over the potatoes and beans and toss gently to combine.

Apricot and chilli meatballs

Preparation time:

20 mins

Cooking time:

20 mins

SERVES 6

1 kg (2 lb 4 oz) minced (ground) pork and veal

250 g (9 oz) dried apricots, chopped

2 tablespoons sweet chilli sauce

80 g (1 bunch) mint, chopped

juice and finely grated zest of 1 small lemon

2 cloves garlic, finely chopped

2 teaspoons garam marsala

salt and freshly ground black pepper

2 tablespoons olive oil

Dipping sauce

160 g ($\frac{1}{2}$ cup) lemon and lime marmalade

125 ml ($\frac{1}{2}$ cup) soy sauce

1   Put the meat, apricots, chilli sauce, mint, lemon zest and juice, garlic and garam marsala in a bowl. Season with salt and pepper. Mix with your hands until well combined.

2   Using a one-third cup as a measure (alternatively, use 4 tablespoons), form the mince mixture into balls and flatten slightly. Heat 1 tablespoon of the oil in a large, heavy-based frypan. Add half of the meatballs and cook over a medium-low heat on each side for 4–5 minutes. Remove and set aside. Add the remaining oil to the pan and cook the second batch of meatballs for 4–5 minutes on each side.

3   Put the marmalade into a small bowl, pour in the soy sauce and mix with a fork to combine. Serve the meatballs with the dipping sauce.

Lamb with cranberry and rosemary

Preparation time:

10 mins

Cooking time:

50 mins plus
10 mins standing

COOK'S TIP

An Easy Carve leg of lamb has had the large bone removed and the small shank bone left intact. A small, tunnel-boned leg of lamb can be used in its place.

SERVES 6

1 Easy Carve leg of lamb (see Cook's tip)

190 g (²/₃ cup) whole berry cranberry sauce

105 g (¼ cup) orange marmalade

2 tablespoons teriyaki sauce

20 g (½ cup) sprigs rosemary, roughly chopped

extra sprigs rosemary, to garnish

1   Remove the string from the lamb leg. Trim away any excess fat, if desired. Make a few slashes in the skin side of the leg. Put the leg on an oven tray skin side down. Combine the cranberry sauce, marmalade, teriyaki sauce and rosemary in a small bowl, stirring well.

2   Cook the lamb for 20 minutes under a preheated medium grill (broiler). Spread with half of the cranberry mixture and cook for 5 minutes longer. Turn the lamb over and cook for a further 20 minutes. Spread with the remaining cranberry mix and cook for 5–10 minutes longer. Leave the leg to stand for 10 minutes and then slice thinly. Garnish with extra rosemary.

Carrot, coriander and pine nut salad

Preparation time:	SERVES 6
10 mins	6 carrots
	90 g (1 bunch) coriander (cilantro)
Cooking time:	70 g (2½ oz) pine nuts, toasted
nil	80 ml (⅓ cup) white-wine vinegar
	juice and finely grated zest of 1 lime
	1 tablespoon soft brown sugar

1 Peel and grate the carrots and place in a large bowl. Add the coriander leaves and pine nuts and toss to combine. Put the vinegar, lime juice, lime zest and brown sugar in a small jug and whisk together with a fork.

2 Pour the dressing over the salad just before serving. Toss gently to combine.

Chocolate yum yums

Preparation time:

15 mins

Cooking time:

25 mins

MAKES 24 BISCUITS

175 g (6 oz) unsalted butter, softened

115 g (½ cup) caster (superfine) sugar

1 teaspoon vanilla essence

185 g (1½ cups) self-raising flour

1 tablespoon cocoa

10 g (⅓ cup) flaked corn breakfast cereal

1 tablespoon shredded coconut

125 g (1 cup) icing (confectioners') sugar

extra 30 g (¼ cup) cocoa

1   Preheat the oven to 160°C (310°F/Gas 2). Line two baking trays with baking paper. Put the butter and sugar in a small bowl and beat with electric beaters until the butter is pale and creamy. Add the vanilla essence and beat for 1 minute longer. Transfer to a large bowl.

2   Sift the flour and cocoa into the same bowl, then add the flaked corn cereal and coconut and mix with a wooden spoon until well combined. Roll tablespoons of the mixture into balls. Position the balls well apart on the prepared trays and press down gently with a fork. Bake for 20–25 minutes. Remove from the oven and leave to cool on the trays, then transfer to a wire rack to cool completely.

3   Sift the icing sugar and extra cocoa into a bowl, make a well in the centre and add enough cold water to form a firm paste. Drop a teaspoon of icing on the top of each cooled biscuit. Leave for 10–15 minutes to set.

Caramel pecan slice

Preparation time:	SERVES 4
20 mins	210 g (1²/₃ cups) plain (all-purpose) flour
	1 teaspoon ground nutmeg
Cooking time:	1 teaspoon baking powder
40 mins	125 g (4¹/₂ oz) butter, chilled and chopped
	3–4 tablespoons cold water
	1 teaspoon vanilla essence
	400 g (14 oz) sweetened condensed milk
	125 g (4¹/₂ oz) butter, chopped
	80 g (¹/₃ cup) caster (superfine) sugar
	60 g (¹/₃ cup) golden syrup
	2 teaspoons vanilla essence
	200 g (7 oz) pecans, roughly chopped

1 Preheat the oven to 200°C (400°F/Gas 6). Line a 30 x 20 cm (12 x 8 inch) tin with baking paper. Sift the flour, nutmeg and baking powder into a food processor. Add the chopped butter and process for 1–2 minutes or until the mixture resembles fine breadcrumbs.

2 Add the water and vanilla essence and process until the mixture just comes together in a ball. Roll the pastry out between two sheets of baking paper to fit the base of the tin. Lift the pastry into the tin and press gently with your hand. Prick the pastry with a fork. Bake for 20 minutes or until golden brown. Remove from the oven. Reduce the oven temperature to 180°C (350°F/Gas 4).

3 Put the condensed milk, butter, sugar, golden syrup and vanilla essence in a heavy-based pan. Stir over a low heat until the sugar dissolves and the mixture is smooth. Cook, stirring, for 10–15 minutes or until the mixture is a pale caramel colour. Add the pecans and stir to combine.

4 Pour the caramel mixture over the prepared base. Return the slice to the oven and cook for 15–20 minutes. Stand on a wire rack to cool before cutting into squares.

Raspberry cordial

Preparation time:

10 mins plus

24 hours standing

Cooking time:

5 mins

COOK'S TIP

To clean your cordial bottle, thoroughly wash it in hot, soapy water and rinse well with hot water. Dry in a 120°C (250°F/ Gas 1/2) oven for 20 minutes.

MAKES ABOUT 375 ml (1 1/2 cups)

300 g (10 1/2 oz) frozen raspberries

1 teaspoon citric acid

185 ml (3/4 cup) water

220 g (1 cup) sugar

1   Put the raspberries into a medium-sized ceramic or glass bowl and allow to thaw. Put the citric acid and water into a jug and stir to combine. Pour this mixture over the thawed raspberries, cover with plastic wrap and allow to stand for 24 hours.

2   Strain the raspberry liquid through a fine sieve into a pan. Do not squash down the fruit as this will produce a cloudy cordial. Add the sugar and stir over a low heat until the sugar is dissolved. Do not boil as this will destroy the flavour and lessen the bright red colour. Cool and pour into a sterilized bottle.

All
wrapped up

Wraps can be loosely defined as any food base that you fill, roll or fold, then pick up with your fingers to eat. They make for an easy-to-serve, fully contained meal you can serve at any time. Just about every cuisine, from Asian to Lebanese to Mexican, features some kind of wrap, and most of the ingredients are now available in supermarkets. The recipes on the following pages will get you started – be adventurous and create your own tasty combinations.

Vietnamese rice paper rolls

These Vietnamese rice paper rolls reflect the fresh, light flavours of their country of origin. Instead of making them all yourself, it can be fun to have your guests fill and roll their own individual rolls. Lay out the rice paper wraps, a bowl of warm water for softening the rice paper and all the trimmings in separate bowls on the table and let each person make their own.

Lots of wraps

Once you start looking, you'll realise how many different kinds of wraps there are available. Nori seaweed is available in most Asian grocery and some larger supermarkets. A 28 g (1 oz) packet contains 10 sheets. Vietnamese rice paper can be purchased from most supermarkets and Asian grocery stores. There are two sizes available and both are suitable for the Vietnamese rice paper rolls.

You will find spring roll wrappers in the freezer section of the supermarket. Take them from the freezer 20 minutes before using. And yes, they should be stretchy.

Whatever type you choose, a good wrap is something the hungry hordes roll up for.

California rolls

Preparation time:

30 mins

Cooking time:

15 mins

COOK'S TIP

Bamboo mats are available
at Asian food stores. They are
inexpensive and indispensable
for making sushi.

MAKES 6 ROLLS

600 g (3 cups) short-grain rice

750 ml (3 cups) water

60 ml (¼ cup) rice vinegar

1 tablespoon mirin or dry sherry

2 tablespoons sugar

2 teaspoons salt

6 sheets nori seaweed

18 cooked king prawns (shrimp), peeled and deveined

10 seafood or crabsticks

2 Lebanese (short) cucumbers, cut into thin strips

1 large avocado, thinly sliced

50 g (1¾ oz) lumpfish caviar

wasabi paste

soy sauce

1 Put the rice in a medium-sized, heavy-based pan. Cover with the water. Bring slowly to the boil, then reduce the heat and simmer, uncovered, until the water evaporates and tunnels appear in rice. Cover, then reduce the heat to very low and cook for 8 minutes.

2 Put the rice vinegar, mirin, sugar and salt into a small pan. Cook over a low heat, stirring continuously until the sugar dissolves. Allow to cool.

3 Gently fork the vinegar mixture through the rice. Spread the rice evenly over the base of a large, flat ceramic dish and allow to cool to room temperature. Cover with a clean, damp cloth.

4 Put a sheet of nori, shiny side down, onto a bamboo mat or sheet of baking paper. With damp hands, spread 150 g (¾ cup) of rice evenly over the nori, leaving a 3 cm (1¼ inch) border free of rice on the far end.

5 Make a hollow in the rice around 3 cm (1¼ inch) in from the edge of the nori and across from left to right. Place 2–3 prawns, a crabstick, some cucumber and avocado over this hollow. Using the mat to help, press firmly and roll. Remove the mat. Leave the roll whole, cut in half or in slices and serve with lumpfish caviar, wasabi paste and soy sauce.

Vietnamese rice paper rolls

Preparation time:

25 mins

Cooking time:

15 mins

MAKES ABOUT 12 ROLLS

1 pork fillet (about 300 g/10½ oz)

1 lime, sliced

2 cm (¾ inch) piece lemon grass

3 cm (1¼ inch) piece ginger

1 teaspoon salt

250 ml (1 cup) cold water

300 g (10½ oz) peeled raw prawns (shrimp), halved lengthways

100 g (3½ oz) rice vermicelli noodles

12 rice paper wrappers

40 g (½ bunch) mint, leaves only

60 g (½ bunch) holy (Thai) basil, leaves only

½ packet bean sprouts, tails removed (see Cook's tip)

1 butter lettuce, washed and patted dry

150 g (1 bunch) garlic chives

Dipping sauce

170 ml (⅔ cup) hoisin sauce

90 g (⅓ cup) smooth peanut butter

1–2 tablespoons boiling water

40 g (¼ cup) chopped roasted, salted peanuts
   and extra, for serving

COOK'S TIP

Bean sprouts tend to go slimy when stored. The best way to keep them fresh is to take them out of the packet, put them in a glass bowl, cover with cold water and keep them in the fridge. They should last for up to five days.

1   Put the pork, lime, lemon grass, ginger and salt in a medium-sized pan. Add the water, cover, bring slowly to the boil and simmer for 10 minutes. Put a single layer of prawns in a steamer and place over the simmering pork for 2–3 minutes. Take the prawns out and set aside. Remove the pork and cut into thin slices.

2   Put the noodles in a pan, cover with warm water and cook for 5 minutes. Drain, rinse with cold water and place in a bowl.

3   Half-fill a large bowl with warm water. Dip one wrapper into the water for 30 seconds. Pat dry with paper towel. Repeat with a second wrapper, and lay it on top of the first. Put two prawn halves at one edge of the rice paper, top with a few slices of pork, some noodles, mint, basil, bean sprouts, lettuce and garlic chives. Roll up tightly, folding the edges in to form a firm, neat roll. Put on a tray, cover with a clean, damp cloth and repeat with remaining rice papers and filling. Serve with the dipping sauce.

4   To make the sauce, put all the ingredients in a small pan and stir over a medium heat until warm. Spoon into a serving bowl, top with peanuts.

Enchiladas with corn and capsicum relish

Preparation time:

25 mins

Cooking time:

50 mins

COOK'S TIP

There are heaps of other
Mexican-style wraps, like crispy
taco shells, in the supermarket –
these can be used instead of
tortillas, if you wish.

SERVES 4

3 large red capsicums (peppers), quartered

1 fresh cob corn

2 red chillies

80 ml (1/3 cup) olive oil

3 cloves garlic, finely chopped

1 small onion, finely chopped

1 tablespoon ground coriander

110 g (1/2 cup) white sugar

250 ml (1 cup) white vinegar

juice of 1 lemon

2 teaspoons salt

2 large chicken breast fillets

40 g (1 1/2 oz) butter

extra 2 large onions, cut into thin wedges

2 tablespoons soft brown sugar

280 g (10 oz) corn tortillas (see Cook's tip)

coriander (cilantro) leaves

1 Remove the membrane and seeds from the capsicums and the husk and silk from the corn. Put them and the chillies onto a baking tray lined with baking paper. Brush with a little oil. Cook under a hot grill (broiler) until the capsicums and chillies have blackened skin. Cool slightly, then peel the skin off the capsicums and chillies. Roughly chop the flesh. Run a sharp knife down the corn to remove the kernels.

2 Heat 1 tablespoon oil in a medium-sized pan. Add the garlic and chopped onion. Cook, stirring occasionally, for 2–3 minutes. Add the capsicums, chillies, corn, ground coriander, white sugar, vinegar, lemon juice and salt. Stir well. Bring slowly to the boil, then reduce the heat and simmer for 20 minutes. Scoop into a bowl.

3 In the same pan heat another tablespoon of the oil. Add the chicken fillets and cook over a medium heat for 5–6 minutes. Turn and cook for 2–3 minutes more. Remove and rest for 10 minutes, covered. Thinly slice, then keep warm.

4 Melt the butter and remaining oil in the pan. Add the onion and brown sugar. Cook over a medium heat, stirring occasionally, for 15–20 minutes or until golden and caramelized. Heat the tortillas according to the instructions on the packet, then fill them with a little each of the chicken, relish and onion. Top with coriander leaves.

Indian dosas with tandoori lamb

Preparation time:	SERVES 4
25 mins plus	750 g (1 lb 10 oz) lamb backstraps or loin fillet
30 mins standing	125 g (½ cup) tandoori paste
	250 g (2 cups) semolina
Cooking time:	30 g (¼ cup) plain (all-purpose) flour
35 mins	185 g (¾ cup) thick plain yoghurt
	310 ml (1¼ cups) water
	2 teaspoons salt, plus extra, for sprinkling
	extra 60 ml (¼ cup) water
	60 ml (¼ cup) oil
	80 g (1 bunch) fresh mint, leaves finely chopped
	1 Lebanese (short) cucumber, finely chopped
	extra 250 g (1 cup) thick plain yoghurt
	extra 1 teaspoon salt

1 Put the lamb in a ceramic or glass heatproof dish. Brush with tandoori paste and allow to stand for 30 minutes. Preheat the oven to 200°C (400°F/Gas 6). Bake the lamb for 20–25 minutes or until cooked through. Remove and allow to stand for 10 minutes before slicing thinly across the grain.

2 Mix the semolina, flour, yoghurt, water and salt in a food processor until well combined. Pour into a medium-sized bowl. Cover with plastic wrap and stand at room temperature for 30 minutes.

3 Add 60 ml (¼ cup) cold water to the semolina mixture and stir to combine. Heat a heavy-based pan. Brush with 1 tablespoon oil and sprinkle with salt. Wipe out the hot pan with paper towel.

4 Pour ¼ cup (3 tablespoons) of the batter into the pan. Spread thinly with the back of a large spoon. Sprinkle with oil and cook for 1–2 minutes. Remove from the pan. Cook the remaining batter in the same way. Keep the dosas warm in a low oven.

5 Combine the mint, cucumber, extra yoghurt and extra salt in a small bowl. Serve the dosas filled with lamb and mint yoghurt.

Salmon and egg noodle spring rolls

Preparation time:

10 mins

Cooking time:

10 mins

COOK'S TIP

These crispy fried rolls are best eaten as soon as they are cooked.

MAKES 15 ROLLS

200 g (7 oz) smoked salmon, finely chopped

150 g (5 1/2 oz) fresh egg noodles

2 spring onions (scallions), thinly sliced

2 tablespoons pickled ginger, finely chopped

50 g (1 3/4 oz) snowpeas (mangetout), thinly sliced

15 spring roll pastry wrappers, thawed

peanut oil

Dipping sauce

juice of 2 lemons

2 tablespoons soy sauce

2 teaspoons sesame oil

2 tablespoons pickled ginger, finely chopped

1 Combine the salmon, noodles, spring onions, ginger and snowpeas in a bowl. Place one spring roll pastry wrapper on the bench and put 2 tablespoons of filling a little in from one corner. Fold the corner over the filling. Brush the other corners with cold water, roll up firmly and press to seal. Repeat using the remaining filling and sheets.

2 Fill a pan one-third full of oil and heat over a medium–high heat until a piece of spring roll wrapper dropped into the oil sizzles. Deep-fry the spring rolls, 3–4 at a time, for 3–4 minutes or until golden brown. Drain and serve immediately with the dipping sauce.

3 To make the sauce, combine the lemon juice, soy sauce, sesame oil and ginger in a small bowl. Stir until well combined.

Sunday brunch

Food for friends

Brunch, that rather decadent combination of breakfast and lunch, is a wonderful way to entertain. By its nature brunch is a casual meal – it allows quality catch-up time for everyone. And if you follow the timetable with this menu, you won't be left out of the fun. Don't forget to have the Sunday papers ready for browsing and maybe a bottle of bubbly on hand to add fizz to the jugs of icy-cold orange juice.

MENU

Homemade Apricot and almond muesli is a must for anyone who can't start the day without a bowl of cereal – just add yoghurt or milk. Next, serve omelettes straight from the pan with a spoonful of Fresh tomato sauce. Hash browns are perfect with lashings of crispy prosciutto or slices of smoked salmon and a dollop of sour cream. Hearty Fetta and spinach muffins are packed full of good tasty things. End the morning with the sweet taste of Flapjacks with roasted strawberries.

Breezy brunch

This brunch menu is a breeze because much of it can be prepared ahead of time. The muesli can be made a month beforehand and kept in a glass jar in the fridge. The muffins can be made a week ahead of time and stored in the freezer (thaw them the night before the brunch). And the Fresh tomato sauce can be made the day before you need it. First thing in the morning on the day of the brunch, make the flapjack mixture and squeeze oranges for fresh orange juice. About half an hour before serving, heat the muffins in a slow oven and cook the prosciutto or bacon and keep it warm. Then all that's left to do is to make the hash browns and omelettes (cook these just before serving because they don't keep well) and cook the flapjacks with strawberries.

A delicious brunch, a lazy Sunday morning, a group of good friends – what a perfect way to start the day!

Fetta and spinach muffins

Preparation time:

15 mins

Cooking time:

25 mins

COOK'S TIP

Texas-size muffins are larger
than traditional muffins. If you
use smaller tins, reduce the
cooking time.

MAKES 12 TEXAS-SIZE MUFFINS

paper muffin cases

310 ml (1 1/4 cups) milk

80 ml (1/3 cup) olive oil

125 g (4 1/2 oz) grated Cheddar cheese

50 g (1 3/4 oz) grated Parmesan cheese

500 g (1 bunch) English spinach, leaves finely chopped

1 tablespoon sweet chilli sauce

3 eggs

375 g (3 cups) plain (all-purpose) flour

4 teaspoons baking powder

1/2 teaspoon salt

200 g (7 oz) fetta cheese, cut into 12 cubes

1 Preheat the oven to 180°C (350°F/Gas 4). Line 12 Texas-muffin moulds with paper cases. Combine the milk, oil, Cheddar cheese, Parmesan cheese, spinach, chilli sauce and eggs in a bowl.

2 Sift the flour, baking powder and salt into a large bowl. Add the milk and cheese mixture and stir with a fork until just combined. Do not over mix.

3 Spoon about 90 g (1/3 cup) of the batter into each mould. Top with a cube of fetta, then more mixture until the moulds are two-thirds filled.

4 Bake for 20–25 minutes or until cooked through when tested with a skewer. Remove from the muffin trays immediately and cool on a wire rack.

Apricot and almond muesli

Preparation time:

10 mins

Cooking time:

15 mins

MAKES 10–12 SERVINGS

400 g (4 cups) rolled oats

60 g (2 cups) rye flakes

55 g (1 cup) shredded coconut

45 g (1/2 cup) wheat germ

15 g (1/2 cup) bran flakes

350 g (1 cup) honey

185 g (1 cup) dried apricots, chopped

80 g (1/2 cup) almonds, chopped

yoghurt and honey, for serving

1 Preheat the oven to 180°C (350°F/Gas 4). Lightly grease a baking dish. Mix the oats, rye flakes, coconut, wheat germ and bran flakes together in a large bowl. Scoop the mixture out onto a baking tray and spread flat. Pour over the honey, then bake for 15 minutes, turning once.

2 Stir the apricots and almonds into the toasted mixture. Set it aside to allow it to cool completely.

3 Serve the muesli with yoghurt and a drizzling of honey, or milk, if you prefer.

Flapjacks with roasted strawberries

Preparation time:

15 mins

Cooking time:

20 mins

MAKES 20–24 FLAPJACKS

2 teaspoons white vinegar

375 ml (1 1/2 cups) milk

250 g (2 cups) self-raising flour

55 g (1/4 cup) caster (superfine) sugar

1 teaspoon bicarbonate of soda

2 eggs

125 g (4 1/2 oz) butter, melted and cooled

750 g (3 punnets) strawberries, hulled and halved

95 g (1/2 cup) soft brown sugar

1 tablespoon vanilla essence

extra butter, for greasing

1 Whisk the vinegar into the milk, then set aside for 10 minutes. Put the flour, sugar, bicarbonate of soda, eggs and milk mixture in a bowl and beat for 3 minutes. Pour in the melted butter and beat for a further 1 minute.

2 Preheat the oven to 200°C (400°F/Gas 6). Put the strawberries in an ovenproof dish. Sprinkle with sugar and vanilla. Bake for 10–15 minutes or until slightly softened and the skin becomes a darker red.

3 While the strawberries are cooking, lightly brush the base of a frypan with extra melted butter. Using a 1/3 cup as a measure (alternatively, use 4 tablespoons), pour batter into the frypan. Cook over a medium heat for 3 minutes or until surface bubbles burst. Flip over and cook the other side until set. Remove from the pan and repeat with the remaining batter. Stack flapjacks on plates and spoon over some strawberries to serve.

Hash browns

Preparation time:	SERVES 4
20 mins	4 large sebago potatoes
	sea salt flakes
Cooking time:	freshly ground black pepper
20 mins	60 g (2¼ oz) butter
	60 ml (¼ cup) oil
	fried 200 g (7 oz) prosciutto or bacon, for serving

1 Preheat the oven to 120°C (250°F/Gas ½). Place a baking tray in the oven. Wash, peel and grate the potatoes. Put the grated flesh into a colander and, using your hands, squeeze out as much liquid from the potatoes as possible. Transfer the flesh to a large bowl. Season with salt and pepper and stir until well combined.

2 Melt 25 g (1 oz) butter with 1 tablespoon oil in a large non-stick frypan. When the butter is sizzling, add three ½ cup quantities (6 tablespoons) of potatoes to the pan to give you three hash browns. Cook, uncovered, for 4–5 minutes on each side or until golden brown and crisp. Transfer to the heated baking tray and place in the oven to keep warm. Cook two more batches of the mixture in this way, adding oil and butter for each batch. Serve with crispy fried prosciutto or bacon.

Individual omelettes with fresh tomato sauce

Preparation time:

10 mins

Cooking time:

15 mins

SERVES 4

Fresh tomato sauce

30 g (1 oz) unsalted butter

1 onion, peeled and roughly chopped

6 medium-ripe tomatoes, roughly chopped

pinch each of sugar, salt and freshly ground
   black pepper

Omelettes

60 g (2¼ oz) unsalted butter, cut into 4 even pieces

8 eggs

chives and parsley, finely chopped

1   To make the Fresh tomato sauce, heat the butter in a heavy-based pan, then cook the onion on a low heat until soft. Add the tomatoes, sugar, salt and pepper. Cook for 10–15 minutes until the tomatoes are soft.

2   For each omelette heat one piece of the butter in a small pan. Thoroughly beat 2 eggs in a small bowl.

3   When the butter is foaming, pour in the egg mixture and reduce the heat to low. Cook, moving the egg mixture from the outside to the centre, until the egg is golden brown and set underneath, but still a little creamy in the centre.

4   Sprinkle the cooked egg with herbs. Fold the omelette in half and tilt the pan to transfer the omelette to a heated plate. Repeat with the remaining butter and eggs. Serve with Fresh tomato sauce.

Spring lunch

Food for friends

Here's the perfect menu for a spring lunch. It's perfect because it uses readily available seasonal ingredients and because it's such a cinch to cook, the whole family can pitch in, even the kids. So, if you're planning a big gathering of family and friends, you can delegate different tasks and lighten the chief cook's load.

MENU

A bowl of Pea soup makes a wonderful start to Sunday lunch. Garnish the soup with a little sprig of mint and serve it with a crusty slice of home-baked Cheese bread. Next, serve up a generous slab of mouth-watering Snapper pie. All it needs to accompany it are tender Steamed vegetables in herb butter and Stuffed tomatoes. Finish on a sweet note with a slice of Orange crème caramel with its topping of liqueur-drenched oranges.

A meal you can cook in advance

If you can't get the extra hands to help, the good news is, you can prepare much of this menu well in advance. Take the Pea soup, it can be made up to two days before serving. And although the Cheese bread is best eaten on the day of baking, it freezes very well. Make sure you give it at least 24 hours to thaw in the fridge and remember to take it out in plenty of time so you can reheat it. The Orange crème caramel dessert can also be made up to two days ahead and should be kept in the fridge. Make sure you cover it well with plastic wrap.

For a quirky touch, serve soup in a teacup instead of a bowl.

Pea soup

Preparation time:	SERVES 8
10 mins	30 g (1 oz) butter
	3 spring onions (scallions), chopped
Cooking time:	40 g (½ bunch) mint, roughly chopped
20 mins	3 large zucchini (courgettes), grated
	400 g (14 oz) peas, fresh or frozen
	1 litre (4 cups) vegetable stock or water
	extra 40 g (½ bunch) mint, for serving
	300 g (10½ oz) thick plain yoghurt

1 Heat the butter in a large pan until it is just melted. Add the spring onion, mint and zucchini, then stir to combine. Cover and cook over a low heat for 8–10 minutes.

2 Add the peas, stir well, then cook for 2–3 minutes. Pour in the stock, cover with a lid, bring slowly to the boil and cook for 5 minutes or until the peas are just tender.

3 Remove the pan from the heat and stand to cool for 5 minutes. Process or blend until the mixture is smooth. Finely chop the extra mint leaves, reserving a few small leaves for garnishing.

4 Put the yoghurt in a small bowl. Add the chopped mint and stir until well combined. Serve the soup in a cup or small soup bowl. Top with a spoonful of the mint and yoghurt mixture and garnish with a mint leaf. Serve a slice of Cheese bread (page 89) on the side.

Cheese bread

Preparation time:

10 mins

Cooking time:

30 mins

SERVES 8

250 g (2 cups) plain (all-purpose) flour

1 tablespoon caster (superfine) sugar

2 teaspoons baking powder

1 teaspoon salt

1/2 teaspoon ground white pepper

60 g (2¼ oz) butter, cut into cubes

250 g (2 cups) grated Cheddar cheese

2 spring onions (scallions), thinly sliced

1 egg

250 ml (1 cup) milk

1 Preheat the oven to 200°C (400°F/Gas 6). Lightly grease a large loaf tin and line the base and sides with baking paper. Put the flour, sugar, baking powder, salt and pepper into a food processor. Add the cubes of butter to the dry ingredients and process until the mixture is like fine breadcrumbs. Transfer the mixture to a large bowl, add the cheese and spring onion and stir until combined.

2 Whisk together the egg and milk. Make a well in the centre of the dry ingredients. Add the combined milk and egg and mix with a table knife to form a soft dough. Do not over mix.

3 Scoop the mixture evenly into the prepared loaf tin. Bake for 30–40 minutes or until the bread is golden and sounds hollow when tapped. Remove from the oven and stand on a wire rack in the tin for 5 minutes before turning out. Cut into slices before serving.

Stuffed tomatoes

Preparation time:

15 mins

Cooking time:

25 mins

SERVES 8

10–12 vine-ripened tomatoes

1 tablespoon oil

1 small onion, finely chopped

150 g (1½ cups) fresh breadcrumbs

45 g (½ cup) grated Parmesan cheese

7 g (⅓ bunch) thyme

salt and freshly ground black pepper

Preheat the oven to 200°C (400°F/Gas 6). Slice the top one-quarter of the tomatoes off to make lids. Remove the pulp from the body of the tomatoes with a teaspoon. Discard the pulp. Heat the oil in a small pan. Add the onion and cook for about 2 minutes or until soft and transparent. Transfer the onion to a small bowl, add the breadcrumbs, cheese, thyme, salt and pepper, then mix well. Spoon the mixture into the tomatoes, sit the lids on top and bake for 15–20 minutes or until tender.

Steamed vegetables with herb butter

Preparation time:

10 mins

Cooking time:

15 mins

SERVES 8

100 g (3½ oz) butter, softened

15 g (¼ cup) finely chopped parsley

15 g (¼ cup) finely chopped basil

1 tablespoon thyme leaves

finely grated zest and juice of 1 small lemon

335 g (1 bunch) baby (Dutch) carrots

10 spring onions (scallions), trimmed with roots left on

150 g (5½ oz) baby green beans

200 g (7 oz) small brussels sprouts

155 g (1 bunch) asparagus, trimmed

Combine the butter, herbs, zest and juice. Scoop onto a sheet of baking paper and roll into a sausage shape. Refrigerate until firm. Fill a large pan one-third of water. Boil, reduce to a simmer, and cook the vegetables until tender. Drain, then put on a platter. Slice the herb butter, sit on top of the hot vegetables and serve.

Stuffed tomatoes

Steamed vegetables with herb butter

Snapper pie

Preparation time:

20 mins

Cooking time:

1 hour

SERVES 8

60 g (2¼ oz) butter

1 large leek, trimmed, washed and sliced

30 g (¼ cup) plain (all-purpose) flour

500 ml (2 cups) fish or vegetable stock

1 small lemon, sliced

125 g (½ cup) cream

salt and ground white pepper

1 kg (2 lb 4 oz) snapper fillets, cut into pieces
    about 8 cm (3 inches) square

375 g (13 oz) ready-made puff pastry

1 egg, lightly beaten

1   Heat the butter in a large pan. Add the leek and cook for 4–5 minutes
    or until tender. Remove the pan from the heat. Add the flour and stir to
    combine. Return the pan to the heat, then cook, stirring, over medium heat
    for 1–2 minutes. Again remove the pan from the heat and slowly pour in the
    stock, stirring continuously until well combined. Return to the heat and stir
    continuously until the sauce comes to the boil.

2   Add the sliced lemon to the sauce, reduce the heat and simmer, uncovered,
    for 10 minutes. Pour the cream into the sauce and stir until well combined
    and heated through. Season with salt and pepper. Put the fish pieces into a
    2 litre (8 cup) oval ovenproof dish. Pour the leek sauce over the fish.

3   Preheat the oven to 200°C (400°F/Gas 6). Place the pastry between two
    sheets of baking paper. Roll the pastry out to a rectangle that is about
    2.5 mm (⅛ inch) in thickness. Trim the pastry to 1 cm (½ inch) from the
    outer edge to make an oval shape. Lay the pastry on top of the dish, folding
    in the edges to form a double edge.

4   To decorate the pie, make small roses and leaves from the pastry trimmings.
    Brush the pie top with egg, then make two small cuts in the top to let steam
    escape. Bake for 30–35 minutes or until the pastry is golden brown and flaky.
    Serve immediately with Stuffed tomatoes and Steamed vegetables with herb
    butter (page 90).

Orange crème caramel

Preparation time:

20 mins plus overnight refrigeration

Cooking time:

1 hour

SERVES 8

80 ml (1/3 cup) water

220 g (1 cup) sugar

250 ml (1 cup) milk

300 ml (10 1/2 fl oz) cream

3 eggs

3 egg yolks

80 g (1/3 cup) caster (superfine) sugar

finely grated zest of 2 oranges

1 teaspoon vanilla essence

1/2 teaspoon orange blossom water (see Cook's tip)

extra 4 oranges

60 ml (1/4 cup) orange liqueur or brandy

1 Preheat the oven to 160°C (310°F/Gas 2). Lightly grease a deep, 23 cm (9 inch) round tin. Put the water and sugar in a medium-sized pan, then stir over a low heat until the sugar dissolves. Bring slowly to the boil, reduce to a simmer and cook for 15–20 minutes or until golden.

2 Remove the toffee from the heat and stand on a heatproof surface until the bubbles subside. Wearing an oven mitt, carefully pour the toffee into the base of the prepared tin. Allow to stand and set.

3 Heat the milk and cream in a small pan until almost boiling. Remove from the heat and stand until lukewarm. Combine the eggs, egg yolks, sugar, orange zest, vanilla and orange blossom water in a mixing bowl. Beat with a whisk until thick and pale yellow. Pour the creamy milk into the egg mixture and whisk to combine.

4 Pour the egg mixture over the toffee. Stand the tin in a deep baking dish. Pour in hot water to come halfway up the sides of the tin. Bake for 40 minutes or until set, then remove the tin from the hot water immediately. Cool and refrigerate for at least 8 hours before serving.

5 Remove the skin and pith from the oranges; this includes the two that have the zest removed and the four extras. Cut into thick slices, then put the slices in a bowl. Pour over the liqueur. Cover and refrigerate until required. Just before serving, upturn the crème caramel onto a large plate and top with orange slices.

Summer

summer food

The longer, warmer days mean more time outside, more leisure and, hopefully, fewer hours in the kitchen for the chef. The foods of summer allow us to do this, so we've taken some of the best seasonal produce and turned it into simple, tasty and refreshing meals that are sure to be a hit.

Asparagus

Green asparagus is available from early spring to mid-winter, but you may also see purple and white varieties at the height of the season. These are prepared in the same way as the green. Choose spears that are crisp and firm and of similar thickness. Store asparagus in the vegetable crisper, but don't wash it before storing. It will keep for 2–3 days but is best used as soon as you get it home.

Snap the tough end off thick spears – just hold one end in each hand and snap; the asparagus will break naturally, leaving you with the tender part. Discard the tough end.

Peaches

Nothing compares with the aroma of this fuzzy-skinned summer fruit, but it must be ripe to have the best flavour, texture and scent. Peaches come in white and yellow varieties and as freestone and clingstone. Freestone peaches are better for use in cooking as the flesh comes away from the stone more easily. Choose firm fruit with no blemishes or bruising. If you need to refrigerate peaches, bring them back to room temperature before eating.

Honeydew melon

Although honeydew melon is available most of the year, it's at its best in the summer months, when it makes a refreshing addition to the summer menu. When buying, look for a melon with unblemished skin and no soft spots. It should feel heavy for its size and have a sweet, aromatic smell. Honeydew melons have their best flavour when very ripe; under-ripe melons can be almost tasteless. Uncut melons can be stored at room temperature. Once cut, however, they're best covered with plastic wrap as their strong aroma may taint other foods. Try placing wedges in the freezer for about 30 minutes for a refreshing treat.

Purple asparagus turns green when cooked.

Chickpea dip

Preparation time:

5 mins

Cooking time:

nil

SERVES 8

440 g (1 lb) can chickpeas, drained

80 ml (1/3 cup) olive oil

juice and grated zest of 1 lemon

2 cloves garlic, peeled

1/2 teaspoon salt

1 teaspoon olive oil

1/2 teaspoon sweet paprika

Put the chickpeas, oil, juice, zest, garlic and salt in a food processor and whiz until smooth. Transfer to a bowl. Drizzle with oil and sprinkle with paprika.

Beetroot dip

Preparation time:

5 mins

Cooking time:

nil

SERVES 8

400 g (14 oz) can baby beetroot, well drained

300 ml (10½ fl oz) plain thick yoghurt

a little chopped mint

Put the beetroot in a food processor and whiz until smooth. Add the yoghurt and stir well. Transfer to a serving bowl and top with mint.

Bread fingers

Preparation time:

5 mins

Cooking time:

20 mins

4 slices lavash bread

1 loaf Turkish bread

olive oil

sea salt

paprika

Line two baking trays with baking paper. Cut the bread into pieces about 5 x 8 cm (2 x 3 inches). Put on the tray, brush with a little oil and sprinkle with salt and paprika. Bake in a 180°C (350°F/Gas 4) oven for 15–20 minutes or until crisp and golden brown. Stand for 10 minutes or until cool. Serve with the Chickpea dip and Beetroot dip.

Prawn and melon salad

Preparation time:

25 mins

Cooking time:

nil

COOK'S TIP

Fresh prawns should have a
pleasant sea smell. The shells
should be smooth and glossy,
firm and intact. Avoid prawns that
have dark discolouration around
the head and legs. Store them in
a glass bowl covered with paper,
then plastic wrap. Refrigerate and
use within 24 hours.

SERVES 4

3 Lebanese (short) cucumbers

1 teaspoon salt

1 small honeydew melon

1 kg (2 lb 4 oz) medium-sized cooked prawns (shrimp),
   peeled and deveined, with tails intact (see Cook's tip)

60 ml (¼ cup) white-wine vinegar

60 g (¼ cup) sweet chilli sauce

grated zest and juice of 1 lime

55 g (¼ cup) pickled ginger

1 Cut the cucumbers into slices on the diagonal. Stack 2–3 slices and cut into strips. Repeat until all the cucumber has been sliced. Put the strips in a bowl, add the salt and mix to combine. Set aside for 20 minutes. Rinse in cold water and pat dry with paper towel.

2 Cut the melon in half and remove the seeds and skin. Cut into thin wedges, then cut each wedge into pieces. Place in a large bowl with half the cucumber and all of the prawns.

3 Put the vinegar, chilli sauce, lime juice and zest in a small bowl or jug, then stir with a fork to combine. Add the dressing to the salad just before serving and toss together. To serve, top with the remaining cucumber strips and the pickled ginger.

Warm asparagus and egg salad

Preparation time:	**SERVES 4**
10 mins	4 eggs
	125 g (4¼ oz) can chickpeas, drained
Cooking time:	60 ml (¼ cup) red-wine vinegar
10 mins	60 ml (¼ cup) olive oil
	1 clove garlic
	465–620 g (3–4 bunches) asparagus, trimmed
	extra 1 teaspoon olive oil
	8 thin slices prosciutto

1 Put the eggs in a pan, cover with cold water and bring slowly to the boil. Reduce to a simmer and cook for 8 minutes. Drain, then cover with cold water. Gently tap each shell to crack it, but leave the shells on. Leave the eggs in the cold water for 5 minutes.

2 Put the chickpeas, vinegar, olive oil and garlic in a food processor and whiz until smooth. Place the asparagus on a grill tray and brush with the extra oil. Cook under a preheated grill (broiler) for 1–2 minutes.

3 Arrange the asparagus on a plate. Peel and cut the eggs in half and place on top of the spears. Spoon the chickpea dressing over the salad and top with the prosciutto.

Ham and crab rolls

Preparation time:	SERVES 4
20 mins	1 large iceberg lettuce
	1 tablespoon olive oil
Cooking time:	250 g (9 oz) leg ham, roughly chopped
10 mins	8 cm (3 inch) piece fresh ginger, peeled and
	cut into slivers
	340 g (12 oz) canned or fresh crab meat
	230 g (8 oz) can water chestnuts, drained and sliced
	230 g (8 oz) canned bamboo shoots, sliced
	60 ml (¼ cup) soy sauce
	1 teaspoon sesame oil
	4 spring onions (scallions), sliced on the diagonal
	2 tablespoons sesame seeds, toasted

1   Wash the lettuce, then remove the core. Cut the lettuce in half and gently peel away the leaves from each half. Place the lettuce cups in a clean, dry tea towel and refrigerate until required.

2   Heat the oil in a large pan. Add the ham and cook, stirring, for 2–3 minutes or until it starts to brown. Add the ginger, crab meat, water chestnuts and bamboo shoots. Stir well and cook, stirring, for 4–5 minutes. Add the soy sauce and sesame oil. Stir to combine and cook for 1 minute longer.

3   To serve, spoon the ham and crab mixture into the lettuce cups, top with some spring onions and sprinkle with the sesame seeds.

Roasted bread and tomato salad

Preparation time:

20 mins

Cooking time:

10 mins

SERVES 4

6 large slices Italian bread

2 tablespoons olive oil

2 cloves garlic, finely chopped

2 Lebanese (short) cucumbers

8 ripe Roma (plum) tomatoes

1 red capsicum (pepper)

125 ml (1/2 cup) olive oil

80 ml (1/3 cup) red-wine vinegar

100 g (3 1/2 oz) black olives, pitted and finely chopped

1 tablespoon chopped rosemary

1   Preheat the oven to 180°C (350°F/Gas 4). Line a baking tray with baking paper. Brush both sides of the bread with olive oil, place on the tray and sprinkle with the chopped garlic. Cook for 10 minutes or until the bread turns pale, golden brown.

2   Chop the cucumbers, tomatoes and capsicum into 1 cm (1/2 inch) cubes. Place in a large bowl. Break the toast into pieces, then add to the cucumber mixture. Put the oil, vinegar, olives and rosemary in a small bowl and whisk to combine. Pour this mixture over the bread and leave to stand for 10 minutes before tossing the salad together. Serve immediately.

Parmesan-crusted chicken with chilli avocado

Preparation time:

20 mins

Cooking time:

20 mins

SERVES 6

6 slices white bread

100 g (1 cup) grated Parmesan cheese

finely grated zest and juice of 2 lemons

salt and freshly ground black pepper

6 small chicken breast fillets, trimmed

Avocado and chilli salsa

2 avocados, finely chopped

1 red onion, chopped

1 green chilli, finely chopped

2 tablespoons red-wine vinegar

2 tablespoons olive oil

salad greens, for serving

1 Preheat the oven to 200°C (400°F/Gas 6). Line a baking tray with baking paper. Put the bread in a food processor and whiz until chunky breadcrumbs form. Turn the crumbs out onto a sheet of baking paper, add the Parmesan, lemon zest, salt and pepper, and mix to combine.

2 Pour the lemon juice into a shallow dish. Dip the chicken breasts in the juice, then roll them in the breadcrumb mixture. Use your hands to press on the crumbs. Lay the coated breasts on the prepared tray. Bake for 15–20 minutes or until cooked through and the crumbs are crisp and brown. Serve topped with the salsa and accompanied by salad greens.

3 For the avocado and chilli salsa, combine the avocado, onion, chilli, vinegar and olive oil in a small bowl.

Caramelized onion tart

Preparation time:

25 mins

Cooking time:

25 mins

Don't be put off by the quantity of onions. They will become sweet and tender due to the sugar and the long cooking time.

SERVES 4

1 tablespoon olive oil

6 onions, thinly sliced (see Cook's tip)

2 tablespoons soft brown sugar

16 slices white bread

90 g (3¼ oz) butter, melted

300 g (10½ oz) sour cream

3 eggs

130 g (1 cup) grated Gruyère cheese

1 Preheat the oven to 200°C (400°F/Gas 6). Line the base of a 23 cm (9 inch) springform tin with a layer of baking paper.

2 Heat the oil in a large, heavy-based pan. Add the onions and sugar and cook over a low heat for 20 minutes, stirring until the onions soften and caramelize.

3 Remove the crusts from each slice of bread. Brush each slice on both sides with melted butter. Arrange the slices slightly overlapping around the springform tin. Place the remaining slices in the base of the tin. Gently press on the bread to seal the edges.

4 Spoon the onions evenly over the bread base. Place the sour cream, eggs and cheese in a medium-sized bowl and beat with a whisk to combine. Pour the sour cream mixture over the onions. Bake for 20–25 minutes or until golden brown and the sour cream mixture is set. Serve warm or cold.

Spaghetti with roasted crumbs

Preparation time:	**SERVES 4**
15 mins	8 slices Italian Vienna bread, roughly chopped
	125 ml (½ cup) olive oil
Cooking time:	4 cloves garlic, finely chopped
20 mins	2 x 45 g (1½ oz) cans anchovies, drained, finely chopped
	60 g (½ cup) capers, finely chopped
	150 g (1 bunch) flat-leaf (Italian) parsley, finely chopped
	500 g (1 lb 2 oz) spaghetti

1 Put the bread in a food processor and whiz until coarse crumbs form. Heat the oil in a large, heavy-based pan. Add the crumbs and cook over a low heat, stirring, for 20 minutes or until the crumbs are golden brown and crisp. Add the garlic, anchovies, capers and parsley. Stir to combine and cook for 1 minute longer.

2 Cook the pasta in a large quantity of boiling, salted water until just tender. Drain, reserving a small jug of the cooking water. Add the crumb mixture to the spaghetti and enough of the cooking water to moisten, then toss to combine. Serve immediately.

Barbecued prawns

Preparation time:

30 mins plus

15 mins marinating

Cooking time:

6 mins

SERVES 4

Marinade 1

2 tablespoons sweet paprika

1 teaspoon ground cardamom

1 teaspoon ground cumin

1 teaspoon ground coriander

1 teaspoon ground ginger

1/2 teaspoon ground cinnamon

1/2 teaspoon chilli flakes

1/2 teaspoon ground black pepper

2 tablespoons olive oil

zest and juice of 1 lime

Marinade 2

shredded zest and juice of 2 limes

80 ml (1/3 cup) olive oil

3 cloves garlic, finely chopped

salt and pepper, to taste

1 kg (2 lb 4 oz) large raw prawns (shrimp), peeled and
   deveined, with tails intact

30 bamboo skewers soaked in cold water for 30 minutes

salad, for serving

1   To make Marinade 1, combine the paprika, cardamom, cumin, coriander,
    ginger, cinnamon, chilli flakes and pepper in a small bowl and stir well.
    Add the olive oil, juice and zest to the spices and mix well.

2   Place all the Marinade 2 ingredients in a small bowl and stir to combine.

3   Thread each prawn lengthways onto the end of each skewer, leaving the tail
    at the end.

4   Place half of the prawn sticks in a bowl. Pour over Marinade 1, turning the
    prawns to coat. Place the remaining prawn sticks in a second bowl and coat
    with Marinade 2. Cook on a hot barbecue for 2–3 minutes per side. Serve
    with a salad.

Marsala mango with macaroon cream

Preparation time:	SERVES 4
10 mins	300 ml (10½ fl oz) cream, softly whipped
	200 g (7 oz) mascarpone
	1 tablespoon icing (confectioners') sugar
Cooking time:	2 teaspoons vanilla essence
5 mins	2 tablespoons sweet Marsala
	½ packet coconut or almond macaroons, crumbled
	4 mangoes
	extra 80 ml (⅓ cup) sweet Marsala
	2 tablespoons soft brown sugar

1 Place the cream, mascarpone, icing sugar, vanilla essence, Marsala and macaroons in a large bowl. Use a large metal spoon to fold in until just combined.

2 Cut the cheeks from each mango and score them in a diamond pattern. Splash each cheek with extra Marsala and sprinkle with brown sugar. Cook flesh-side down on a hot barbecue plate for 3–4 minutes.

3 Serve the mangoes with a spoonful of the macaroon cream.

Brown-bread and mango cake

Preparation time:

25 mins

Cooking time:

40 mins

SERVES 6

8 slices wholemeal bread

125 g (4½ oz) slivered almonds

2 teaspoons ground cinnamon

6 eggs

2 teaspoons vanilla essence

185 g (1½ cups) icing (confectioners') sugar, sifted

1 mango, peeled and roughly chopped

extra freshly sliced mango, for serving

lightly whipped cream, for serving

pulp of 4 passionfruit, for serving

1   Preheat the oven to 180°C (350°F/Gas 4). Line the base and sides of a deep, round 23 cm (9 inch) cake tin with a sheet of baking paper. Put the bread, almonds and cinnamon in a food processor and whiz until fine breadcrumbs form. Transfer to a large bowl.

2   Put the eggs and vanilla essence in a large bowl and use electric beaters to beat on high for about 15 minutes or until the egg mixture becomes thick and turns pale yellow.

3   Add the icing sugar and mango to the breadcrumb mixture. Using a large metal spoon, fold these together until they are just combined; take care not to over mix. Spoon the mixture into the prepared cake tin. Bake for 35–40 minutes or until the cake is firm to the touch and starts to shrink away from the sides of the tin.

4   Take the cake out of the oven and let it stand on a wire rack for 10 minutes. Turn the cake out of the tin and leave it to cool. Serve the cake with the extra slices of mango, whipped cream and passionfruit pulp.

Roasted peaches with pistachio ice cream

Preparation time:

25 mins plus freezing

Cooking time:

10 mins

SERVES 4

1 litre (4 cups) thick plain yoghurt

1/2 teaspoon cardamom seeds

115 g (1/3 cup) honey

2 teaspoons vanilla essence

125 g (41/2 oz) pistachio kernels

45 g (1/2 cup) desiccated coconut

4 peaches

1 teaspoon ground cardamom

extra 2 tablespoons honey

1 Put the yoghurt, cardamom seeds, honey and vanilla in a bowl and stir together. Transfer to a loaf tin, cover with plastic wrap and place in the freezer for 2–3 hours or until the mixture starts to set.

2 Scoop the yoghurt mixture into a food processor, add the pistachios and coconut and process until the pistachios are finely chopped. Return the mixture to the loaf tin, cover with plastic wrap and put in the freezer for several hours or overnight.

3 Preheat the oven to 200°C (400°F/Gas 6). Line a baking tray with baking paper. Cut each peach in half and remove the stone. Arrange the halves on the tray. Place the ground cardamom and extra honey in a small bowl and stir to combine. Drizzle the honey mixture over the peaches. Bake the peaches for 10 minutes or until just tender.

4 Serve the peaches warm, accompanied by a scoop of the pistachio ice cream.

Peach Melba

Preparation time:	SERVES 8
25 mins	750 ml (3 cups) water
	1 vanilla bean, split
Cooking time:	495 g (2¼ cups) sugar
40 mins	8 medium-firm, ripe peaches
	300 g (10½ oz) fresh or frozen raspberries
	extra fresh raspberries (optional)

Step 1
Put the water, vanilla bean and sugar in a large, deep, heavy-based pan. Place over a low heat and stir continuously until the sugar dissolves. Bring the sugar mixture slowly to the boil. Boil for 3 minutes, then reduce to a very low simmer and cook, covered, for 4–5 minutes.

Step 2
Carefully add the peaches to the syrup and simmer, covered, for 10–15 minutes or until the peaches are just tender. Use a slotted spoon to remove the peaches from the syrup. Place on an oven tray lined with baking paper. Bring the syrup slowly to the boil. Reduce to a simmer and cook, uncovered, for 20 minutes.

Step 3
To make the raspberry sauce, place the raspberries and 250 ml (1 cup) of the syrup in a food processor and whiz until the mixture is smooth.

Step 4
Prick the top of each peach with the point of a small knife to loosen the skin. Pull the skin down and away from each peach. Place the peaches in a serving bowl. Pour over 250 ml (1 cup) of the remaining syrup. Serve with the raspberry sauce and a few fresh raspberries, if desired.

Pineapple and coconut upside-down cake

Preparation time:

25 mins

Cooking time:

55 mins

SERVES 8

1 small pineapple, crown, skin and eyes removed

90 g (3¼ oz) butter

115 g (½ cup) caster (superfine) sugar

finely grated zest and juice of 1 lime

extra 125 g (4½ oz) butter, chopped

2 teaspoons coconut essence

extra 230 g (1 cup) caster (superfine) sugar

2 eggs

185 g (1½ cups) self-raising flour, sifted

90 g (1½ cups) shredded coconut

125 ml (½ cup) coconut milk

Palm sugar cream

300 ml (10½ fl oz) cream

60 g (⅓ cup) grated palm sugar

1 Preheat the oven to 180°C (350°F/Gas 4). Lightly grease a deep 23 cm (9 inch) round tin and line the base and sides with baking paper. Cut the pineapple flesh into thin wedges, remove the core and roughly chop.

2 Put the butter, sugar, lime zest and juice in a small pan and stir over a low heat until the sugar dissolves. Bring slowly to the boil, then reduce to a simmer and cook for 1–2 minutes. Pour into the prepared tin, then add the pineapple to the tin.

3 Put the extra butter and the coconut essence in a small bowl and, using electric beaters, beat on high until the butter increases in volume. Add the sugar and beat until the mixture is light and fluffy. Add the eggs, one at a time, beating well between each addition. Transfer the batter to a large bowl. Add half each of the flour, coconut and coconut milk and stir with a large metal spoon until just combined. Add the remaining flour, coconut and coconut milk and stir well. Spoon the batter evenly over the pineapple and then smooth the surface. Bake for 50–55 minutes or until a skewer comes out clean when inserted in the centre. Stand the tin on a wire rack for 20 minutes before carefully turning out. Serve the cake warm with Palm sugar cream.

4 To make the Palm sugar cream, put the cream and palm sugar in a small pan and stir over a medium heat until the sugar melts. Pour the mixture into a mixing bowl and refrigerate until well chilled, then whip the cream until just thick.

Sugar-topped grilled pineapple

Preparation time:

5 mins

Cooking time:

5 mins

SERVES 6–8

1 pineapple

90 g (3¼ oz) butter

230 g (1 cup) dark brown sugar

1 tablespoon vanilla essence

vanilla ice cream, for serving

1 Remove the crown from the pineapple and slice off the top but leave the skin on. Cut the pineapple into wedges, then cut each wedge into slices.

2 Beat the butter, brown sugar and vanilla essence together with electric beaters until combined.

3 Place the pineapple on a foil-lined tray and put a spoonful of the butter mixture onto each pineapple wedge. Cook under a preheated grill (broiler) for 2–3 minutes. Serve hot with scoops of vanilla ice cream.

Chocolate-dipped cherries

Little cherry meringues

Chocolate-dipped cherries

Preparation time:

5 mins

Cooking time:

5 mins

MAKES 24 CHERRIES

250 g (9 oz) chocolate (either use all dark chocolate, or
use one-third each of dark, milk and white chocolate)

24 cherries

Cover a baking tray with baking paper. Put each chocolate into a separate small heatproof bowl. Sit the bowl over a pan of simmering water, without letting the bowl touch the water. Stir the chocolate continuously until it is melted and smooth. Remove from the heat. Dip the bottom half of each cherry in the chocolate and place on the baking tray to set. Serve with coffee.

Little cherry meringues

Preparation time:

15 mins

Cooking time:

30 mins

MAKES 12–15 MERINGUES

2 egg whites

115 g (½ cup) caster (superfine) sugar

12–15 cherries

Preheat the oven to 160°C (310°F/Gas 2). Line a baking tray with baking paper. Put the egg whites and sugar into a small clean, dry bowl and beat with electric beaters on low for 3 minutes. Increase to high and beat for another 8–10 minutes until the mixture is thick and glossy. Place teaspoons of the mixture onto the baking tray. Carefully sit a cherry in the centre of each meringue. Bake for 25–30 minutes or until the meringue is crisp. Turn the oven off and leave the trays in the oven to cool.

Summer
seafood feast

Summer's here and the sea, sand and sun are calling. But if you can't make it to the beach, you can still get into the spirit of the season with a seafood feast at home. This banquet nets a bounty of the freshest seafood and casts around seasonal produce for a spread that's ideal for a summer's day.

MENU

This menu can be served two ways, as a series of courses or laid out as a buffet. If you want to serve the meal dish by dish, start with the Oyster shots with frozen margarita and then those in the shells. Next, serve the Salmon gravlax and Potato with prosciutto and Prawns and scallops with radicchio and witlof with an assortment of salads. If you'd rather keep things informal, let your guests help themselves. Follow the main course with a spectacular fruit jelly. The base is ginger ale, which has a subtle tang that teams well with the strawberries and grapes. If you don't have a scalloped mould, serve the jelly in individual glasses.

Enjoy these summer delicacies outside in the summer shade.

Choosing and storing seafood

- Ideally, oysters should be bought live, with the shell closed. It should be heavy and full of water. Look for plump, glossy oysters that smell fresh.
- Choose fresh prawns with a pleasant smell, and firm shells. Avoid any that smell of ammonia or with dark discolouration around the head or legs – this means they are starting to deteriorate.
- Scallops should have a fresh and pleasant sea smell.
- Salmon can be wild or farmed. Wild fish are generally superior in flavour and less fatty than farmed fish.
- Remember that any seafood, cooked or raw, must not be left to stand at room temperature for longer than half an hour. Keep it in the fridge until the last minute, refrigerate leftovers as soon as possible and eat within 24 hours.

Oyster shots with frozen margarita

Preparation time:

15 mins plus
several hours freezing

Cooking time:

nil

COOK'S TIP

The tequila and Cointreau
shots have quite a kick. For a
refreshing, non-alcoholic
variation, use lime juice as a
base and add an ordinary
ice cube. Chill in the fridge
instead of the freezer.

MAKES 8 SHOTS

juice of 3 limes

125 ml (1/2 cup) tequila

60 ml (1/4 cup) Cointreau

extra 60 ml (1/4 cup) lime juice

1 lime, halved

sea salt flakes

8 freshly shucked oysters

1 Pour the lime juice into a 12-hole ice cube tray, top up with water and freeze.
Pour the tequila, Cointreau and extra lime juice into a cocktail shaker or
screw-top jar. Shake well, then pour into a bar tin. Cover with plastic wrap
and place in the freezer until firm. The mixture will not freeze solid because
of the high alcohol level, but it will become slushy.

2 Put eight shot glasses in the freezer to chill. Grind the rim of each glass into
the cut lime and then into sea salt flakes to give an encrusted rim. Place a
lime ice cube in each glass. Spoon the tequila slush into the glasses and
top with an oyster.

Oysters with ginger and cucumber

Preparation time:	MAKES 8 OYSTERS
10 mins	2 tablespoons pickled pink ginger, finely chopped
	1 small Lebanese (short) cucumber
Cooking time:	8 large oysters in the shell
nil	finely grated zest of 1 small lemon
	sea salt flakes
	freshly ground black pepper

Put the pickled ginger in a small bowl. Peel the cucumber, cut it in half lengthways, and scoop out the seeds. Finely chop the flesh and put it in a small bowl. Place the oysters on a platter lined with rock salt to keep them stable. Top each with a little ginger, cucumber and lemon zest. Sprinkle with sea salt and freshly ground black pepper.

Oysters with pink chilli mayo

Preparation time:	MAKES 8 OYSTERS
10 mins	125 g (¼ cup) whole-egg mayonnaise
	2 teaspoons sweet chilli sauce
Cooking time:	1 teaspoon tomato sauce
nil	sea salt flakes
	white pepper
	8 oysters in the shell
	2 iceberg lettuce leaves, finely shredded
	1 chilli, seeded and sliced

Put the mayonnaise, sweet chilli sauce, tomato sauce, salt and pepper in a small bowl. Stir until well combined. Remove the oysters from their shells and sprinkle a little lettuce into each shell. Sit the oysters on the lettuce. Add a dollop of the Pink chilli mayo and serve garnished with thinly sliced chilli.

Prawns and scallops with radicchio and witlof

Preparation time:	**SERVES 8**
25 mins	1 radicchio, cut into thin wedges
	3 witlof (chicory/Belgian endive), cut into thin wedges
Cooking time:	1 kg (2 lb 4 oz) cooked king prawns (shrimp)
15 mins	750 g (1 lb 10 oz) scallops
	60 ml (¼ cup) red-wine vinegar
	2 tablespoons olive oil
	sea salt flakes
	freshly ground black pepper

1 Place the radicchio and witlof on a large serving platter. Cover with plastic wrap and refrigerate until needed. Peel and devein the prawns, leaving the tails intact. Place in a medium-sized bowl, cover with plastic wrap and refrigerate until required.

2 Heat a large non-stick grill pan or barbecue hotplate. Cook the scallops for 1–2 minutes on each side or until golden brown. Place the prawns and scallops onto the bed of leaves.

3 To make the dressing, pour the red-wine vinegar and olive oil into a small bowl. Whisk until well combined. Drizzle the prawns and scallops with the dressing and then sprinkle with salt and pepper. Serve with Chargrilled pineapple and mango salad (page 141).

Chargrilled pineapple and mango salad

Preparation time:	SERVES 8
10 mins	1 small pineapple
	3 mangoes
Cooking time:	2 small red chillies
15 mins	120 g (1 bunch) fresh basil, small leaves only

1 Remove the crown from the pineapple, then cut off the skin and cut out the eyes. Cut out the core, then cut the flesh into long thin wedges

2 Peel the mangoes and cut the flesh into large wedges. Seed the chillies and thinly slice the flesh.

3 Heat a barbecue hot plate or grill pan. Cook the pineapple and mango on the hot plate on each side for 1–2 minutes or until golden. Put in a large bowl and sprinkle with the chilli and small basil leaves.

Salmon gravlax

Preparation time:

15 mins plus
24 hours standing

Cooking time:

nil

SERVES 8

4 tablespoons sea salt flakes

2 tablespoons sugar

1 side fresh salmon

250 g (1 bunch) dill, finely chopped

finely grated zest of 2 lemons

250 g (1 cup) sour cream

3 tablespoons horseradish cream

2 lemons, cut into wedges

Sprinkle sea salt and sugar over the salmon, then press firmly into the fish. Cover with plastic wrap, then a sheet of cardboard and weigh it down with something heavy. Refrigerate for 24 hours. Remove the fish from the refrigerator and wash it under cold running water. Pat dry with paper towel. Put the dill and lime zest in a bowl and mix well. Press the mixture onto the salmon and keep in the fridge until required. Combine the sour cream and horseradish cream in a small bowl and whisk with a fork. Using a sharp knife, cut the salmon into very thin slices. Serve with lemon wedges, the cream mixture and Potato with prosciutto.

Potato with prosciutto

Preparation time:

10 mins

Cooking time:

45 mins

SERVES 8

1 1/2 kg (3 lb 5 oz) desiree potatoes

olive oil

8 slices prosciutto

2 tablespoons white-wine vinegar

1 tablespoon seeded mustard

30 g (1 bunch) chives, finely chopped

Preheat the oven to 220°C (425°F/Gas 7). Cut the potatoes into 1 cm (1/2 inch) slices. Place on two baking trays lined with baking paper. Brush with oil and sprinkle with sea salt. Bake for 40–45 minutes or until golden and crisp. Put the prosciutto on a baking tray and place under a hot grill (broiler). Cook for 5 minutes or until crisp. Turn and cook for a further 1–2 minutes. Remove and cool. Break into pieces. To make the dressing, put 2 tablespoons oil, the vinegar and mustard in a small bowl. Whisk with a fork. Place the potatoes on a platter and sprinkle with prosciutto and chives. Drizzle with the dressing and season.

Avocado and pawpaw salad with sweet lime dressing

Preparation time:

15 mins

Cooking time:

nil

SERVES 8

1 pawpaw

2 avocados

40 g (1/2 bunch) fresh mint, leaves only

3 limes

2 tablespoons caster (superfine) sugar

Remove the skin from the pawpaw, then cut the flesh in half lengthways. Slice into thin wedges and then cut each wedge into chunks and put in a large bowl. Remove the skins and stones from the avocados, then cut the flesh into 2 cm (3/4 inch) cubes and add to the pawpaw. Add the mint leaves. Finely grate or shred the zest of 1 lime. Place in a small bowl. Juice all 3 limes and add to the bowl with the zest. Add the sugar and stir until the sugar dissolves. Add to the pawpaw and avocado. Gently toss.

Cherry tomato and bocconcini salad

Preparation time:

10 mins

Cooking time:

nil

SERVES 8

500 g (2 punnets) cherry tomatoes

350 g (12 oz) baby bocconcini (mozzarella)

45 g (1/2 bunch) fresh coriander (cilantro),
    leaves only

juice of 1 lemon

2 tablespoons olive oil

sea salt flakes

freshly ground black pepper

Wash the tomatoes and place them in a large bowl. Drain the bocconcini and add to the tomatoes. Put the coriander leaves, lemon juice, olive oil, salt and pepper in a small bowl. Whisk with a fork until well combined. Pour over the salad and toss gently.

Ginger ale fruit jelly

Preparation time:

15 mins

plus setting

Cooking time:

nil

SERVES 8

1 teaspoon gelatine

3 tablespoons hot water

80 ml (1/3 cup) boiling water

80 ml (1/3 cup) lemon juice

375 ml (1 1/2 cups) ginger ale

1 tablespoon sugar

500 g (2 punnets) small strawberries

250 g (9 oz) black seedless grapes

250 g (9 oz) red seedless grapes

Ginger cream

300 ml (10 1/2 fl oz) cream

110 g (1/2 cup) glacé ginger, finely chopped

1   Place the gelatine in a small bowl. Add the hot water, stir with a fork to combine, then stand for 5 minutes to soften and swell. Pour the boiling water into a medium-sized mixing bowl. Stir in the softened gelatine and continue stirring until the gelatine dissolves. Stir in the lemon juice, ginger ale and sugar. Set the bowl aside for 1 hour at room temperature, or refrigerate for 30 minutes until the jelly is just beginning to set.

2   Remove the hulls from the strawberries and put the berries in a large bowl with all the grapes. Add the jelly mixture to the fruit and gently fold through with a large metal spoon. Pour into a 1.5 litre (6 cup) mould, cover with plastic wrap and refrigerate until set. Remove the jelly mould from the fridge and dip the base quickly into hot water. Place a serving dish or cake stand over the top of the mould and flip to free the jelly. Serve with a dollop of Ginger cream and a few Coconut wafers (page 149).

3   For the Ginger cream, whip the cream until soft peaks form. Fold in the chopped ginger.

Coconut wafers

Preparation time:	MAKES 5 TRAYS
10 mins	2 egg whites
	115 g (1/2 cup) caster (superfine) sugar
Cooking time:	60 g (2 1/4 oz) butter, melted and cooled
10 mins	1 teaspoon vanilla essence
	1 teaspoon coconut essence
	60 g (1/2 cup) plain (all-purpose) flour
	30 g (1/2 cup) shredded coconut, toasted

1 Preheat the oven to 180°C (350°F/Gas 4). Beat the egg whites and sugar with a fork until smooth. Add the cooled melted butter, vanilla and coconut essence, then sift in the flour. Stir until well combined. Line two baking trays with baking paper. Using a spatula, spread the wafer batter thinly over the trays to cover the whole surface.

2 Sprinkle the batter with toasted coconut. Bake for 8–10 minutes or until golden brown. Remove from the oven and allow to cool completely. Break each biscuit into large pieces and store in an airtight container. The coconut wafers will keep for up to one week.

basil

Basil is the ultimate summer herb. It's the perfect partner for tomatoes, creating a flavour match made in heaven. Basil also stimulates the appetite and aids in digestion – two more good reasons to start using it.

Growing basil

Basil is an annual planted in late spring, so it's at its best at the start of summer. Wherever it's grown, it needs lots of sunshine and plenty of food and water. Pinch off flower heads to encourage bushy growth and try not to pick more than half the plant at any one time or it may go into shock. If you have more basil than you know what to do with, try the pesto and basil-oil recipes on the following pages. Both use a lot of basil and will keep for up to three weeks in the fridge.

Buying, storing and using basil

Basil is available in summer and early autumn. Look for firm, crisp leaves, with no black marks. Basil deteriorates quickly and is best stored with its stalks in water in a cool, dry place. Don't wash it – just wrap it in a paper towel and store in a plastic bag in the fridge. It should last about five days. Leaves can be used whole, roughly chopped or torn. For the best flavour, add it at the end of cooking.

Topping it all off

Crispy fried basil leaves make a special garnish for steamed rice or noodles. Not only do they taste fantastic, they look good, too.

Remove the leaves from a bunch of basil but don't wash them. Heat enough oil to come one-third of the way up the sides of a small, deep, heavy-based pan. When the oil is hot, add just a couple of basil leaves. Stand back – they'll spit a little. Cook for a few seconds, remove from the oil with a slotted spoon and place on a paper towel to drain. Allow to cool, then use immediately.

Even if you don't have a garden, you can still grow basil successfully in pots.

Basil, eggplant and tomato salad

Preparation time:

25 mins

Cooking time:

25 mins

SERVES 4

2 medium-sized eggplants (aubergines), sliced

2 teaspoons salt

60 ml (1/4 cup) olive oil

60 ml (1/4 cup) red-wine vinegar

2 cloves garlic, sliced

4 medium-sized, vine-ripened tomatoes, sliced

1 teaspoon sugar

extra 1 teaspoon salt

200 g (7 oz) fetta cheese, sliced

120 g (1 bunch) basil, leaves only

1 tablespoon olive oil

1   Preheat the oven to 200°C (400°F/Gas 6). Put the eggplant in a bowl, sprinkle with the salt and toss to combine. Leave to stand for 10 minutes. Rinse the eggplant in water and pat dry with paper towel.

2   Pour the oil and vinegar into a small bowl and whisk together. Lay the eggplant slices on a baking tray and sprinkle with the garlic. Pour the oil and vinegar mixture over the eggplant, then bake for 20–25 minutes.

3   Put the sliced tomatoes in a shallow dish. Sprinkle with the sugar and extra salt, cover with plastic wrap and leave to stand for 5 minutes.

4   To serve, layer the eggplant, tomato, fetta and basil in a shallow bowl or plate. Drizzle the extra oil over and sprinkle with a few extra basil leaves.

Prawns and squid with basil

Preparation time:

25 mins

Cooking time:

10 mins

SERVES 4

1/2 teaspoon sea salt flakes

1/2 teaspoon freshly ground black pepper

1/2 teaspoon chilli flakes

500 g (1 lb 2 oz) raw prawns (shrimp)

2 medium-sized squid tubes

2 tablespoons oil

250 ml (1 cup) white wine

120 g (1 bunch) basil, leaves only

1 Put the salt, pepper and chilli flakes in a small dry frypan and cook over a low heat for 2–3 minutes. Transfer to a small bowl and set aside.

2 Peel and devein the prawns, leaving the tail on. Cut the squid tubes in half. Slice each half-tube into 2.5 x 5 cm (1 x 2 inch) strips and crosshatch with the tip of a sharp knife (being careful not to cut all the way through).

3 Heat the oil in a large wok or heavy-based pan. Add the prawns and cook over a high heat until they change colour. Remove from the oil and set aside. Add the squid and cook for 3–4 minutes. Remove and set aside while you make the sauce.

4 Add the wine to the wok or pan. Bring to the boil and boil for 2–3 minutes or until reduced by half. Return the prawns and squid to the pan. Toss to combine and coat in the sauce. Add the salt mixture and basil leaves. Toss to combine, then serve immediately.

Basil oil

Preparation time:
10 mins

Cooking time:
nil

MAKES ABOUT 410 ML (1²/₃ CUPS)

120 g (1 bunch) basil, leaves only

250–375 ml (1–1¹/₂ cups) virgin olive oil

2 cloves garlic

Put the basil leaves in a food processor. Add the oil and garlic. Process until the mixture is smooth, then pour into a clean, dry jar or bottle. It will keep in the fridge for up to 3 weeks. Use it to flavour pasta, to pour over steamed potatoes or to drizzle over steamed salmon.

Roasted almond and basil pesto

Preparation time:
10 mins

Cooking time:
nil

MAKES ABOUT 625 G (2¹/₂ CUPS)

250 g (9 oz) roasted almonds

120 g (1 bunch) basil, leaves only

100 g (1 cup) grated Parmesan cheese

2 cloves garlic

185 ml (³/₄ cup) olive oil

Put the almonds, basil leaves, grated Parmesan, garlic and olive oil in a food processor. Process until the nuts are finely chopped and the mixture is well combined. Spoon into a clean, dry jar. Cover the surface with a thin layer of oil to prevent the pesto from discolouring.

Basil oil

Roasted almond and basil pesto

Basil and pineapple sorbet

Preparation time:

20 mins plus
several hours freezing

Cooking time:

20 mins

SERVES 4

1 medium-sized pineapple

330 g (1 1/2 cups) sugar

250 ml (1 cup) water

120 g (1 bunch) basil, leaves only

Sugared basil leaves

1 egg white

a few extra basil leaves

a little sugar

1   Peel the pineapple and cut in quarters. Remove the core from each quarter, then chop the fruit roughly. Set aside.

2   Put the sugar and water in a medium-sized, heavy-based pan. Stir over a low heat until the sugar is dissolved. Bring slowly to the boil, boil for 2–3 minutes, then reduce to a simmer.

3   Add the pineapple and basil leaves to the sugar syrup. Cook, uncovered, over a low heat for 15–20 minutes, then pour into a large loaf tin. Stand to cool for 20 minutes. Cover loosely with plastic wrap. Place in the freezer for several hours or overnight.

4   Put the pineapple mixture in a food processor and whiz until smooth. Serve immediately or return to the freezer, where it will keep for up to 3 days. Top with sugared basil leaves just before serving.

5   For the sugared basil leaves, place the egg white in a small bowl and whisk with a fork until frothy. Brush each basil leaf with a little of the beaten egg white (or do as we have, and only brush half of each leaf). Sprinkle the wet leaves with a little sugar. Place on a paper-lined wire rack and leave to dry.

Tarting it up

When we think of tarts and pies or other pastry dishes, we usually think cool weather. Not any more! Summer's produce can be used to make the most mouth-watering sweet tarts. And the savoury pastry dishes make great-tasting picnic food, starters or even meals. Follow our easy pastry-making tips and start baking.

Blind baking

Blind baking or baking blind simply means that the pastry is precooked before a filling is added. When you bake pastry in this way, it gives a crispy shell and also helps to prevent the pastry from shrinking.

To blind bake, line the pastry with a sheet of greaseproof or baking paper and fill the base with baking beads, dried beans or rice. Baking beads are available from specialty kitchenware shops or department stores.

Pastry-making tips

- Measure all ingredients accurately.
- Plain (all-purpose) flour gives pastry a crisp texture. Self-raising flour gives a spongy, cake-like texture.
- Butter gives the best flavour and makes for a crisp shortcrust.
- Keep ingredients chilled to stop the butter from melting before it's meant to – it should only start to melt in the oven. Keep your hands cold, too, by washing them in chilled water just before you make the pastry.
- Rub the butter into the flour with your fingertips (not palms) or use a food processor.
- The water should be chilled. Add a few ice cubes to a jug of water.
- Don't overknead pastry or you'll make it tough and chewy.
- Let the pastry rest in the fridge between making, rolling and baking to help prevent shrinkage.
- Roll the pastry out on a lightly floured board between sheets of baking paper or plastic wrap.
- Always ease the pastry into the tin. Never stretch it to fit or it will shrink during baking.
- Trim the pastry by running a rolling pin across the top of the pastry in the tin. This cuts the pastry around the edges and it simply drops off.

The secret to kneading pastry is to use your fingertips and the heel of your hand until it comes together.

Zucchini torte

Preparation time:

25 mins plus soaking

Cooking time:

35 mins

SERVES 4

1 kg (2 lb 4 oz) zucchini (courgettes)

1 tablespoon salt

8 sheets filo pastry

60 g (2¼ oz) butter, melted

60 g (½ cup) self-raising flour

75 g (¾ cup) grated Parmesan cheese

pinch of nutmeg

salt and freshly ground black pepper

4 eggs

125 ml (½ cup) olive oil

1   Cut the zucchini into thin slices. Put half the slices in a colander and sprinkle with half the salt. Top with the remaining zucchini slices and sprinkle with the rest of the salt. Stand over a bowl for 2 hours to soften.

2   Preheat the oven to 180°C (350°F/Gas 4). Brush a 23 cm (9 inch) springform tin with melted butter. Fold each filo sheet in half and brush the top of each half with melted butter. Arrange the sheets of pastry so they overlap in the tin – don't trim the edges. Brush with melted butter. Rinse the sliced zucchini under cold water, then pat completely dry with paper towel.

3   Sift the flour into a large bowl and add the Parmesan, nutmeg and salt and pepper in a large bowl and stir to combine. Put the eggs in a small bowl and beat with electric beaters until thick and a pale yellow colour. Add the olive oil, zucchini slices and eggs to the flour mixture. Using a large metal spoon, fold them into the mixture until just combined.

4   Spoon the mixture into the prepared tin and smooth the surface. Cook for 35 minutes or until set, well risen and golden brown. Stand on a wire rack for 10 minutes before removing from the tin.

Tomato tarts

Preparation time:

30 mins

plus standing

Cooking time:

35 mins

COOK'S TIP

These cute little tarts are just the thing for a brunch, summer lunch or even a picnic. Our recipe uses a fresh black olive tapenade but if you're short on time, simply use your favourite bottled version. A rich spicy tomato paste could be substituted for the tapenade if you prefer a tomato flavour.

MAKES 6 TARTS

375 g (3 cups) plain (all-purpose) flour, sifted

125 g (1 cup) grated Romano cheese

1 teaspoon paprika

180 g (6 oz) butter, chilled and chopped

125 ml (1/2 cup) chilled water

1 egg

750 g (1 lb 10 oz) vine-ripened baby tomatoes

olive oil spray or olive oil

sea salt flakes

Tapenade

1 clove garlic, peeled

1/2 teaspoon sea salt flakes

1 tablespoon capers

45 g (1 1/2 oz) can anchovy fillets, rinsed in cold water
    and patted dry

2 teaspoons fresh thyme

135 g (1 cup) black olives, pitted

1   Put the flour, cheese, paprika and butter into a food processor and whiz until the mixture resembles fine breadcrumbs. Add the combined water and egg, and process until the mixture just comes together. Turn onto a lightly floured surface and press into a ball. Wrap in plastic wrap and refrigerate for 20 minutes.

2   Preheat the oven to 180°C (350°F/Gas 4). Line two baking trays with baking paper. Arrange the tomatoes on the trays, spray or brush with olive oil and sprinkle with sea salt flakes. Bake for 10–15 minutes or until the flesh is soft and the skins are starting to shrink. Remove from the oven and stand to cool.

3   For the tapenade, place the garlic, sea salt flakes, capers and anchovy fillets into the bowl of a food processor. Process to a smooth paste. Add the thyme and olives. Process to a paste.

4   Reline the trays with baking paper. Preheat the oven to 200°C (400°F/Gas 6). Divide the pastry into six pieces and knead each into a ball. Roll out each ball to a round 15 cm (6 inches) in diameter. Leaving a border of 4 cm (1 1/2 inches), spread 1 tablespoon of tapenade over the pastry. Place the tomatoes on top, then fold in the edges of the pastry to cover the edge of the tomatoes. Put on the trays and bake for 15–20 minutes or until the pastry is golden.

Egg and salmon tart

Preparation time:

20 mins

Cooking time:

15 mins

COOK'S TIP

Buy salmon roe in bottles from your deli or fishmonger. If it's not available in your area, use a bottle of red or black lumpfish roe. You'll find it in the chiller section of most supermarkets.

SERVES 8

250 g (9 oz) savoury cracker biscuits

125 g (4½ oz) butter, melted and cooled

250 g (9 oz) light cream cheese

60 g (¼ cup) whole-egg mayonnaise

9 eggs, hard-boiled, peeled and cooled

salt and white pepper

300 g (10½ oz) sour cream

100 g (3½ oz) salmon roe, to garnish (see Cook's tip)

dill sprigs, to garnish

1 Preheat the oven to 180°C (350°F/Gas 4). Brush a 23 cm (9 inch), deep, round springform tin with butter. Line the base and sides with baking paper. Put the biscuits in the bowl of a food processor and whiz until fine crumbs form. Transfer the crumbs to a bowl, add the butter and stir until combined. Press the crumbs evenly into the base of the prepared tin, pressing down with the back of a spoon to firm the mixture. Bake for 10–15 minutes. Remove from the oven and stand on a wire rack to cool. Cover with plastic wrap and refrigerate.

2 Put the cream cheese and mayonnaise in the bowl of a food processor and stir together. Add the eggs, salt and pepper and whiz until chopped. Spoon onto the biscuit base and spread evenly. Cover with plastic wrap and refrigerate.

3 Spread the sour cream over the egg mixture. Refrigerate the tart until ready to serve. Before serving, unmould onto a plate and top with salmon roe and sprigs of dill.

Tarte Tatin

Preparation time:

25 mins

Cooking time:

30 mins

SERVES 6

90 g (3$\frac{1}{4}$ oz) unsalted butter

125 g (1 cup) plain (all-purpose) flour

$\frac{1}{2}$ teaspoon baking powder

60–80 ml ($\frac{1}{4}$–$\frac{1}{3}$ cup) chilled water

1 egg yolk

6 medium-sized, just-ripe peaches

165 g ($\frac{3}{4}$ cup) white sugar

extra 30 g (1 oz) butter

3 passionfruit

extra 30 g ($\frac{1}{4}$ cup) plain (all-purpose) flour

rich vanilla ice cream, for serving

1   Cut the butter into small cubes, put into a bowl and chill in the freezer for 5–10 minutes. Sift the flour and baking powder into a mixing bowl. Add the butter and toss to combine. Make a well in the centre. Put the water and egg yolk in a small jug and whisk to combine. Pour into the well in the dry ingredients. Stir with a table knife to form a soft dough.

2   Turn out the dough onto a lightly floured surface and knead gently. Roll out to a rectangle measuring about 15 x 30 cm (6 x 12 inches). Fold the dough into three sections. Gently press down on the edges with a rolling pin. Turn the dough through 90° so the top flap is on your right. Repeat this folding-and-rolling process twice more. Wrap the dough in plastic wrap and refrigerate for 30 minutes.

3   Preheat the oven to 200°C (400°F/Gas 6). Line the base of a 23 cm (9 inch), deep, round tin with baking paper. Wash the peaches, dry gently with paper towel, then cut each peach into quarters. Pour the sugar into a medium non-stick frypan. Cook over medium heat (without stirring) until the sugar melts and turns dark golden. Add the butter and passionfruit pulp and swirl to combine. Pour the mixture into the tin. Arrange the peaches over the passionfruit mix.

4   Roll out the pastry on a lightly floured surface to about 23 cm (9 inches) in diameter. Place the pastry over the peaches, pushing the edges down into the pan. Bake for 25–30 minutes or until the pastry is well risen and dark golden brown. Remove from the oven and stand on a wire rack to cool for 5–10 minutes. Carefully turn out onto a serving plate. Serve in wedges with a scoop of vanilla ice cream on the side.

Summer fruit tart

Preparation time:

30 mins plus

standing

Cooking time:

30 mins

SERVES 6

70 g (½ cup) roasted hazelnuts

250 g (2 cups) plain (all-purpose) flour

1 teaspoon baking powder

2 tablespoons soft brown sugar

1 teaspoon ground cinnamon

125 g (4½ oz) butter, chilled and chopped

4–5 tablespoons chilled water

250 g (9 oz) mascarpone

2 tablespoons icing (confectioners') sugar, sifted

1 teaspoon vanilla essence

315 g (1 cup) apricot jam

50 ml (2 fl oz) Cointreau, optional

250 g (1 punnet) strawberries, hulled and sliced

120 g (4½ oz) fresh raspberries

3 small peaches, stones removed, cut into thin wedges

150 g (5½ oz) blueberries or small currant grapes

1 Finely chop the hazelnuts in a food processor. Add the flour, baking powder, brown sugar and cinnamon. Whiz for 30 seconds to combine, then add the butter and process until the mixture resembles fine breadcrumbs. Add the water and process until the mixture just comes together. Turn onto a lightly floured surface and press into a flat ball. Wrap in plastic wrap and refrigerate for 20 minutes.

2 Preheat the oven to 200°C (400°F/Gas 6). Lightly grease a 31 x 15 x 2 cm (12 x 6 x ¾ inch), loose-bottomed, flan tin. Roll out the pastry to a 5 mm (¼ inch) thick rectangle large enough to fit the base and sides of the tin. Ease the pastry into the tin. Cover with plastic wrap and chill for about 15 minutes.

3 Line the pastry with baking paper and fill with dried beans or rice. Put on a baking tray and bake for 20 minutes. Remove the tin from the oven and carefully take out the paper and beans or rice. Return the tin to the oven and bake the pastry for 10 minutes. Put the tart tin on a wire rack to cool the pastry shell.

4 Put the mascarpone, icing sugar and vanilla in a small bowl. Stir well. Spread into the cold pastry shell with a flat-bladed knife. Refrigerate until firm. Put the jam and Cointreau in a small pan and stir continuously over a medium heat to combine. Bring to the boil, then reduce the heat and simmer for 2–3 minutes. Pour into a fine sieve over a bowl, then push through the sieve. Arrange the fruit over the tart filling and brush with the jam mixture.

Step by Step
Lemon tart

Preparation time:	SERVES 8
25 mins plus	225 g (8 cups) plain (all-purpose) flour, sifted
30 mins chilling	40 g ($\frac{1}{3}$ cup) pure icing (confectioners') sugar, sifted
	185 g (6$\frac{1}{2}$ oz) unsalted butter, chopped and chilled
Cooking time:	1 egg, separated
50 mins	1 tablespoon cold water
	1 teaspoon vanilla essence
	5 eggs
	170 g ($\frac{3}{4}$ cup) caster (superfine) sugar
	125 g ($\frac{1}{2}$ cup) cream
	1 teaspoon vanilla essence
	185 ml ($\frac{3}{4}$ cup) lemon juice
	extra sifted icing sugar, for dusting

Step 1

Preheat the oven to 200°C (400°F/Gas 6). Grease a 28 cm (11 inch) loose-bottom flan tin. Mix the flour, icing sugar and butter in a food processor until the mixture resembles fine breadcrumbs. Add the egg yolk (reserve the white), water and vanilla and process using short bursts just until a ball starts to form. Do not over process.

Step 2

Remove the pastry from the processor and knead gently into a ball. Using your hand, gently flatten the dough. Wrap in baking paper and chill for 15–20 minutes. Roll the pastry out between two sheets of baking paper to a round 2 cm ($\frac{3}{4}$ inch) larger than the tin. Remove the top layer of paper and ease the pastry into the tin; don't stretch the pastry.

Step 3

Trim the edges by pushing a rolling pin over the top. Refrigerate for 10 minutes. Put the tin on a baking tray. Line the pastry with baking paper; fill with rice. Bake for 20 minutes. Remove the paper and rice, then bake for a further 10 minutes. Remove from the oven and cool on a wire rack. Brush with egg white. Reduce the oven to 160°C (310°F/Gas 2).

Step 4

Put the eggs, caster sugar, cream and vanilla in a large bowl; whisk well. Add the lemon juice and whisk until combined. Transfer to a large jug. Pour the filling over the back of a large metal spoon into the pastry shell. Bake for 25 minutes. The centre should still be a little wobbly. Cool on a wire rack. Dust with icing sugar just before serving.

All about
summer
berries

Do you remember picking blackberries when you were a child? They'd grow in the most unlikely places and it was a challenge to be the first to fill your container. The range of berries available today goes well beyond the humble blackberry. We have used strawberries, raspberries and blueberries in the following recipes.

Growing strawberries

Strawberries can be grown in pots, tubs or in the ground. They need a sunny position, well-drained soil and regular feeding and watering. If you grow them in the ground, a surface mulch of grass clippings, compost, straw or pine bark will suppress weeds and maintain an even soil temperature to prevent the plants from drying out. You can get non-running varieties of strawberries that are suitable for pots and tubs. Ask about them at your local nursery.

The best of berries

The berry season extends from mid-spring to mid-autumn but you'll find the best berries in summer. And in very hot summers, they're plump, juicy and sweet. Avoid them at either end of the season, as they can be lacking in flavour and juice.

Buying, storing and preparing strawberries

Berries are available by the punnet from most greengrocers. Check that there's no excess juice in the bottom of the container and no sign of mould. It's best to eat berries on the day you buy them. Refrigeration dulls their flavour so if you have to put them in the fridge, be sure to bring them back to room temperature before serving. They need little preparation, too – just a quick rinse under cold water and a good shake to remove excess moisture, or a gentle pat dry with a paper towel, and they're ready to eat. Always wash your strawberries with the hulls intact to prevent them from becoming waterlogged.

You don't need to be a greenthumb to grow great strawberries.

Strawberry shortcake

Preparation time:

20 mins

Cooking time:

25 mins

SERVES 6

250 g (2 cups) self-raising flour

55 g (1/4 cup) caster (superfine) sugar

90 g (3 1/4 oz) butter, chilled and chopped

2 eggs, separated, whites reserved for glazing

80 ml (1/3 cup) milk

extra caster (superfine) sugar

315 g (1 cup) redcurrant jelly

500 g (2 punnets) small strawberries

1 Preheat the oven to 200°C (400°F/Gas 6). Line a baking tray with baking paper. Sift the flour into a bowl, add the sugar and stir to combine. Rub the butter into the flour with your fingertips until the mixture resembles fine breadcrumbs. Make a well in the centre.

2 Place the egg yolks and milk in a small bowl and whisk with a fork to combine. Pour into the well in the dry ingredients, then use a flat-bladed knife to mix it quickly into a soft dough. If the mixture seems a little bit dry, add another tablespoon of milk.

3 Turn the mix onto a lightly floured surface, knead gently, then press into a 3 cm (1 1/4 inch) thick circle. Brush with egg white and sprinkle with extra sugar. Bake for 25 minutes or until golden. Cool on a wire rack.

4 Spoon the redcurrant jelly into a small pan. Stir over a medium heat until the jelly boils, then boil for 2–3 minutes. Pile the strawberries onto the cake. Pour the jelly over the strawberries. Stand for 10 minutes before serving.

Blueberry and almond friands

Preparation time:

15 mins

Cooking time:

8 mins

MAKES 36 MINI FRIANDS

185 g (6½ oz) butter, chopped

330 g (1½ cups) icing (confectioners') sugar

125 g (1¼ cups) ground almonds

60 g (½ cup) plain (all-purpose) flour

grated zest of 1 orange

5 egg whites

150 g (5½ oz) fresh blueberries (raspberries can be used in place of blueberries for this recipe, if desired)

extra 30 g (¼ cup) plain (all-purpose) flour

extra sifted icing sugar, for dusting, optional

1 Preheat the oven to 200°C (400°F/Gas 6). Lightly grease three 12-hole mini muffin tins (if you don't have three tins, cook them in batches). Melt the butter over low heat, making sure it doesn't brown.

2 Sift the icing sugar into a bowl. Add the almonds, flour and zest. Make a well in the centre, add the egg whites and mix to form a smooth paste. Add the melted butter a little at a time, mixing thoroughly between each addition.

3 Roll the blueberries in a little extra flour. This prevents them from dropping to the base of the friands. Gently fold the blueberries through the batter with a metal spoon.

4 Fill the moulds three-quarters full with batter. Bake for 8–10 minutes or until firm. Leave in the tin for a few minutes, then transfer to a wire rack to cool. Dust with icing sugar just before serving, if desired.

Quick berry jam

Raspberry vinegar

Quick berry jam

Preparation time:

25 mins

Cooking time:

15 mins

MAKES ABOUT 630 G (2 CUPS)

500 g (1 lb 2 oz) fresh berries

330 g (1 1/2 cups) sugar

Sterilize jars by washing them thoroughly in hot, soapy water. Dry them in a 120°C (235°F/Gas 1/2) oven for 20 minutes. Wash and hull the berries, if required. Place the berries and sugar in a large, heavy-based pan. Stir over a medium heat until the sugar dissolves completely. Bring the liquid slowly to the boil, reduce the heat, then let the liquid simmer, uncovered, for 12–15 minutes. Remove from the heat and let cool slightly. Pour the jam into a sterilized jar, then seal.

Raspberry vinegar

Preparation time:

10 mins plus

overnight standing

Cooking time:

15 mins

MAKES ABOUT 1.25 LITRES (5 CUPS)

185 g (1 1/2 cups) raspberries

1.25 litres (5 cups) white-wine vinegar

2 tablespoons caster (superfine) sugar

Put the raspberries into a large glass or ceramic bowl and pour the vinegar over them. Cover with plastic wrap, then leave to stand at room temperature for several hours or overnight. Strain the vinegar into a medium-sized pan using a fine sieve lined with a piece of muslin. Add the sugar to the vinegar and stir to combine. Bring slowly to the boil, reduce to a simmer and cook, uncovered, for 10 minutes. Carefully pour the hot vinegar into sterilized bottles (see Quick berry jam for instructions). Seal and label. Use within 3–4 weeks. Keep the vinegar in the fridge during very hot weather.

Strawberry cordial

Preparation time:

30 mins plus

24 hours standing

Cooking time:

10 mins

MAKES 1 LITRE (4 CUPS)

500 g (2 punnets) strawberries, cut in half

2 teaspoons citric acid

440 g (2 cups) white sugar

1   Put the halved strawberries in a large ceramic or glass bowl. Add the citric acid and 375 ml (1½ cups) water. Cover the berries with plastic wrap and allow to stand for 24 hours.

2   Sterilize bottles by washing them thoroughly in hot, soapy water. Dry them in a 120°C (235°F/Gas ½) oven for 20 minutes.

3   Pour the liquid through a fine sieve lined with muslin into a medium-sized pan. Add the sugar. Stir over a low heat, just until sugar dissolves. Do not allow to boil as this changes the colour of the cordial. Remove from heat, pour into sterilized bottles and refrigerate.

Cold desserts

What better finale to a summer meal than a delicious chilled or frozen dessert? Each recipe in this cool collection is very easy to make and would be great to serve when you're entertaining as each one can be made up to a week in advance. Just keep well covered in the freezer.

Ice cream treats

Make your own Chocolate-coated ice cream balls by using a melon baller or teaspoon to make neat balls of ice cream. Put the balls on a baking tray lined with baking paper and freeze for 3 hours or until they are hard. Melt 250 g (9 oz) dark chocolate and 60 g (2¹/4 oz) copha and melt over low heat. Dip each ice cream ball into the mixture, allowing the excess to drain away. Return to the baking tray or put in a small paper cup. Freeze for several hours, or overnight.

Serving cold desserts

On the day of your party, if the weather is very warm, chill your serving plates in the freezer for about an hour before using. Remove the dessert from the freezer and place in the refrigerator for 10–20 minutes before it's needed. This time in the fridge will allow the dessert to soften just a little, enhancing its flavour and texture. To make neat servings dip your knife, scoop or spoon in a little hot water so you can make a clean cut. Then tuck in and enjoy.

A chilled dessert is the most delicious way to keep your cool this summer.

Zuccotto

Preparation time:

35 mins plus
several hours chilling

Cooking time:

nil

SERVES 8

2 x 350 g (12 oz) Madeira (pound) cakes, loaf-shaped
  (see Cook's tip)

50 ml (2 fl oz) Cointreau

300 g (10$\frac{1}{2}$ oz) fresh ricotta cheese

2 tablespoons icing (confectioners') sugar

1 teaspoon vanilla essence

300 ml (10$\frac{1}{2}$ fl oz) cream, lightly whipped

95 g ($\frac{1}{2}$ cup) mixed peel

200 g (7 oz) good-quality dark chocolate, finely chopped

100 g (3$\frac{1}{2}$ oz) Vienna almonds or toasted almonds,
  chopped

extra 1 tablespoon sifted icing (confectioners') sugar,
  for dusting

1 tablespoon sifted cocoa, for dusting

1 Line a 2 litre (8 cup) pudding basin with plastic wrap. Cut the cake into five long slices (about 1 cm/$\frac{1}{2}$ inch thick), then cut each slice diagonally into two triangles. Fully line the basin with the triangles. Have the narrow end of each piece meeting in the centre of the base of the bowl. The bits sticking out the top can be trimmed after the filling goes in. Splash the cake with Cointreau.

2 Put the ricotta in a bowl. Sift in the icing sugar, add the vanilla and beat with a wooden spoon until the mixture is creamy. Use a large metal spoon to fold the cream through the mixture, then fold in the peel, chocolate and almonds.

3 Spoon the ricotta mixture into the cake-lined basin. Trim the cake to the level of the top of the bowl. Press the remaining cake over the ricotta. Cover with plastic wrap and refrigerate for several hours or overnight.

4 To serve, remove the plastic wrap, invert the zuccotto onto a plate and remove the remaining plastic wrap. Dust with icing sugar and cocoa.

Lime and passionfruit sherbet

Preparation time:

30 mins

plus chilling

Cooking time:

5 mins

SERVES 6

220 g (1 cup) sugar

500 ml (2 cups) milk

grated zest and juice of 4 limes

600 ml (21 fl oz) thickened cream or single cream

250 g (1 cup) passionfruit pulp (about 8 fresh passionfruit)

extra 125 g (½ cup) passionfruit pulp, for serving

1 Place the sugar, milk and lime zest in a medium-sized pan and stir over a low heat until the sugar has dissolved. Remove from the stove and add the lime juice – this will cause the mixture to curdle. Pour into a shallow metal tray or baking tin and keep in the freezer until the edges start to freeze.

2 Line a large loaf tin with baking paper or plastic wrap. Spoon the cream into a large bowl. Beat the cream with a balloon whisk or hand beater until soft peaks form. Remove the lime mixture from the freezer and gently fold it into the cream along with the passionfruit until the ingredients are well combined.

3 Pour the mixture into the prepared tin and return to the freezer. Freeze for several hours or overnight, then remove from the tin and cut into slices. Serve with a drizzle of passionfruit pulp.

Coconut ice cream with lychee sorbet

Preparation time:

25 mins

plus several hours freezing

Cooking time:

10 mins

SERVES 8

3 egg yolks

170 g (3/4 cup) caster (superfine) sugar

2 x 400 ml (14 fl oz) coconut milk

30 g (1/2 cup) shredded coconut, toasted

2 x 565 g (1 lb 4 oz) cans lychees in syrup

1 Put the egg yolks, sugar, and coconut milk in a large bowl. Place the bowl over a simmering pot of water and stir continuously with a wooden spoon until the custard thickens slightly. Remove from the heat and pour the mixture into a large loaf tin. Allow it to cool. Cover the tin with plastic wrap and place in the freezer for several hours or until firm.

2 Remove the coconut mixture from the freezer and put it in a large food processor. Whiz until the mixture is thick and creamy. Put into a large bowl and fold through the toasted coconut using a metal spoon. Return to the loaf tin, cover with plastic wrap and place in freezer for several hours or until frozen.

3 Pour the lychees and syrup in a large food processor and process until the lychees are finely chopped. Pour into a large loaf tin, cover with plastic wrap and place in the freezer for several hours or until frozen. Serve big scoops of the lychee sorbet with coconut ice cream.

Meringue and raspberry cream torte

Preparation time:

10 mins plus
several hours freezing

Cooking time:

nil

SERVES 8

2 kg (4 lb 8 oz) good-quality vanilla and strawberry
    ripple ice cream
300 g (10½ oz) fresh or frozen raspberries
10 ready-made meringue nests, gently crushed
extra 300 g (10½ oz) fresh or frozen raspberries

1   Line a 22 cm (9 inch) round springform cake tin with plastic wrap. Allow the ice cream to soften but not melt. Spoon one-third of the ice cream into the base of the tin, cover with half the raspberries then half of the crushed meringues. Continue to layer the ingredients in this way, ending with a layer of ice-cream. Cover the tin with plastic wrap and then freeze.

2   Remove from the freezer, peel off the plastic wrap and turn out onto a large plate. Top with extra raspberries and cut into wedges to serve.

Chocolate, coffee and hazelnut ice cream loaf

Preparation time:

10 mins plus
several hours freezing

Cooking time:

nil

SERVES 8

300 ml (10½ fl oz) cream, well chilled

1 litre (4 cups) ready-made chocolate custard

60 ml (¼ cup) strong black coffee

125 g (4½ oz) roasted hazelnuts, roughly chopped

Sauce

125 g (4½ oz) dark chocolate

300 ml (10½ fl oz) cream

extra chopped chocolate

1 Beat the cream in a large bowl until soft peaks form. Fold in the chocolate custard and coffee using a large metal spoon. Spoon into a large loaf tin. Cover with plastic wrap and freeze for several hours.

2 Remove the chocolate mixture from the freezer and scoop into the bowl of a large food processor. Process until thick and creamy. Transfer to a large bowl and fold in the hazelnuts using a large metal spoon. Return to the loaf tin, cover with plastic wrap and place in the freezer for several hours.

3 To make the sauce, break the chocolate into pieces and put in a bowl with the cream. Place the bowl over simmering water. Stir continuously until a smooth sauce forms. Remove from the heat. Allow to cool.

4 To serve, turn the loaf out onto a large plate and remove the plastic wrap. Sprinkle with extra chopped chocolate. Cut into slices and serve with the chocolate sauce.

Autumn

Warming
asian soups

One of the best things about autumn and winter in terms of food is being able to tuck into a hot hearty soup. It's the ultimate comfort food and is a great pick-me-up at the end of a long, cold day. The Asian soups on the following pages are very filling and packed with delicacies and wonderful Oriental flavours that you'll love.

How to strain stock

Take out any large pieces of meat and vegetable with a slotted spoon, then stand the stock for 10 minutes. To strain, you'll need a stainless-steel colander as well as a fine, stainless-steel strainer. If you don't have a fine strainer, line your colander with muslin, which is available from fabric stores and speciality kitchenware shops. A clean, well-worn tea towel will also do the job.

How to cook your own stock

Cut a large onion, carrot and a stalk of celery into chunks and put in a large pot with a bouquet garni and extra vegetables, beef, chicken or fish (see below for more information on which ingredients to include).

Cover the ingredients with cold water. Bring slowly to the boil, uncover, then reduce to a simmer.

As your stock simmers, you'll see a foamy scum developing around the edges of the pot. This should be removed with a slotted spoon during the cooking process.

■ For vegetable stock, use carrots, celery, onion and mushroom stalks. Add water and simmer for 1½ hours.

■ For chicken stock, place a meaty carcass or a few chicken pieces in a pot, cover with water and simmer for 1½ hours. Add the vegetables and simmer for an hour.

■ For beef stock, put bones and well-browned pieces of meat in a pot, cover with water, then simmer for 2–3 hours. Add the vegetables and simmer for an hour.

■ For fish stock, place a meaty fish carcass and vegetables in a pot with water and simmer for 45 minutes. Don't overcook as this will give the stock a bitter taste.

It's a good idea to make soup or the stock for your soup the day before serving, to allow the flavours to develop.

Sweet corn and chicken soup

Preparation time:

25 mins

Cooking time:

1½ hours

COOK'S TIP

Serve the soup with Chinese
prawn crackers, which are
available from the Asian section
of many supermarkets.

SERVES 6

1.8 kg (4 lb) chicken, cut in half through the breast
   and back, thoroughly washed

2 carrots, roughly chopped

4 sticks celery, roughly chopped

1 large onion, cut into quarters

10 g (½ bunch) lemon thyme

2 bay leaves

a few white or black peppercorns

2 litres (8 cups) water

1 tablespoon peanut or vegetable oil

4 spring onions (scallions), chopped, plus extra, shredded

8 cm (3 inch) piece ginger, chopped

4 large or 6 medium corn cobs, kernels only

1 tablespoon cornflour (cornstarch) blended with
   60 ml (¼ cup) sweet sherry

60 ml (¼ cup) soy sauce

1 teaspoon sesame oil

1 teaspoon salt

½ teaspoon white pepper

2 egg whites

1 tablespoon cold water

1 Put the chicken in a large, deep, heavy-based pan with the carrots, celery, onion, thyme, bay leaves and peppercorns. Pour in the water. Cover and bring slowly to the boil. Cook for 45 minutes, then lift off the lid and cook for a further 20 minutes. Remove the chicken with tongs and put on a plate to cool. Strain the stock, discarding the solids, then return it to the pan and simmer for a further 10 minutes. Remove the skin from the chicken and shred the meat. Discard the skin and bones.

2 Heat the oil in a pan, add the spring onions, ginger and corn and stir over a medium heat for 5 minutes. Transfer to a food processor and blend until a paste forms.

3 Stir the corn mixture into the stock, add the chicken meat and stir well. Stir the cornflour mixture into the soup and cook, stirring, until it comes to the boil and thickens slightly. Reduce to a simmer. Add the soy sauce and sesame oil and simmer for 15 minutes. Season. Beat the egg whites with the cold water until just starting to foam. Stir the soup to create a whirlpool, then pour in the egg white mixture in a thin steady stream. Serve topped with shredded spring onion.

Prawn laksa

Preparation time:

30 mins

Cooking time:

50 mins

SERVES 4

1 kg (2 lb 4 oz) raw prawns (shrimp)

1 tablespoon oil

3 stalks coriander (cilantro), roots and leaves

1 onion, roughly chopped

2 makrut (kaffir) lime leaves

1 teaspoon salt

6 peppercorns

1 litre (4 cups) water

1 tablespoon oil

250 g (1 cup) ready-made laksa paste

juice of 2 limes

425 g (15 oz) can coconut milk

2 tablespoons fish sauce

200 g (7 oz) vermicelli noodles

1 small red onion, thinly sliced

1 Lebanese (short) cucumber, peeled and thinly sliced

90 g (1 cup) bean sprouts, tails removed

1 Peel and devein the prawns, leaving the tails intact. Retain the heads and shells. Put the prawns in a bowl, cover with plastic wrap and refrigerate until required. Heat the oil in a large pan and add the prawn heads and shells. Cook over a medium heat for 2–3 minutes. Add the coriander, onion, lime leaves, salt and peppercorns. Pour in the water and cook over a low heat for 20 minutes. Remove from the heat and strain through a fine sieve, discarding the solids.

2 Heat the oil in a pan. Add the laksa paste and cook, stirring, for 3–4 minutes. Pour in the stock, lime juice, coconut milk and fish sauce. Bring slowly to the boil, then reduce the heat and simmer for 8–10 minutes.

3 Put the noodles in a large bowl. Cover with boiling water and allow to stand for 4–5 minutes or until soft. Drain and rinse under warm water. Put equal amounts of noodles into four deep soup bowls.

4 Add the prawns to the soup and cook for 4–5 minutes or until the prawns turn pink and are cooked through. Put equal amounts of prawns, onion, cucumber and bean sprouts in the bowls. Ladle the soup into the bowls. To serve, top with snowpea sprouts, mint and fried shallots, if desired.

Beef and vegetable pho

Preparation time:

30 mins plus 20 mins freezing

Cooking time:

55 mins

COOK'S TIPS

To bruise cardamom pods, put the pod on a wooden board and tap gently with a rolling pin so it splits the shell. Thin slices of raw beef are added to the hot stock just before serving; the stock will cook the beef. If you prefer, drop the meat into the stock for as long as you wish, depending on how rare you like your meat.

SERVES 4

350 g (12 oz) rump steak

2 litres (8 cups) beef stock

3 cm (1 1/4 inch) piece fresh ginger

1 cinnamon stick

6 cardamom pods, bruised (see Cook's tips)

4 star anise

2 tablespoons fish sauce

300 g (10 1/2 oz) thick rice noodles

150 g (5 1/2 oz) snowpeas (mangetout)

150 g (5 1/2 oz) baby green beans

2 small fresh button mushrooms, sliced

60 g (1/2 bunch) basil, small leaves only

40 g (1/2 bunch) mint, leaves only

To serve

4 hard-boiled eggs, cut into wedges

125 g (1/2 bunch) coriander (cilantro), leaves only

1 lime, cut into wedges

chilli paste or sauce

extra fish sauce

1 Wrap the meat in plastic wrap and put it in the freezer for 20 minutes or until the meat becomes firm, but not frozen. Put the stock, ginger, cinnamon stick, cardamom pods, star anise and fish sauce in a large, heavy-based pan. Bring slowly to the boil, then reduce the heat and simmer for 20 minutes. Strain the stock and return to the pan, discarding the solids.

2 Put the noodles in a large bowl. Cover with boiling water and allow to stand for 30 minutes or until soft. Remove the meat from the freezer and use a large, sharp knife to cut it into thin slices, across the grain. Put the meat on a plate, cover and allow to thaw completely.

3 Bring the stock to the boil, add the snowpeas, beans and mushrooms and cook for 1 minute. Drain the noodles and divide among four bowls. Add the prepared meat to the bowls. Ladle the hot stock mixture over the noodles. Top with basil and mint. Serve with quartered hard-boiled eggs, coriander, lime wedges, a little chilli paste and fish sauce.

Long and short soup

Preparation time:

30 mins plus

30 mins soaking

Cooking time:

20 mins

COOK'S TIPS

Gow gee wrappers are available
from most supermarkets or
Asian food stores. You can use
won ton wrappers instead.
Fresh or dried egg noodles can
be used in this recipe.

SERVES 6

5 dried Chinese mushrooms

200 g (7 oz) minced (ground) pork

5 whole water chestnuts, finely chopped

1 spring onion (scallion), finely chopped

1 tablespoon oyster sauce

salt and white pepper

1 teaspoon cornflour (cornstarch)

1 tablespoon water

24 gow gee wrappers

1 litre (4 cups) chicken stock

2 litres (8 cups) water

60 ml (1/4 cup) soy sauce

2 teaspoons sesame oil

185 g (6 1/2 oz) thin egg noodles

375 g (1 bunch) baby bok choy (pak choi),
    leaves separated

1   Put the mushrooms in a heatproof bowl. Cover with boiling water and soak
    for 30 minutes or until soft. Drain and chop finely. Put in a medium-sized
    bowl. Add the pork, water chestnuts, spring onion, oyster sauce and some
    salt and pepper. Stir until well combined.

2   Put the cornflour and water in a small bowl and stir together. Place three
    gow gee wrappers on a flat surface. Put a teaspoon of pork mixture in the
    middle of each one, then brush the edges with the cornflour mixture. Bring
    the corners up and press together to form a sack shape. Continue filling the
    gow gee wrappers, three at a time, until all the ingredients are used.

3   Pour the stock and water into a pan. Slowly bring to the boil. Add the gow
    gees and cook for 3–4 minutes. Add the soy sauce, sesame oil and noodles
    and cook for 1–2 minutes. Just before serving, add the bok choy.

Miso soup with salmon and asparagus

Preparation time:

15 mins

Cooking time:

5 mins

Miso is a paste made from fermented soya beans with other flavourings. Generally, the lighter the colour, the milder the flavour.

SERVES 4

200 g (7 oz) sliced smoked salmon or smoked trout

55 g (2 oz) pickled ginger

1 tablespoon wasabi paste

60 g (1/4 cup) white miso paste (see Cook's tip)

500 ml (2 cups) fish stock

1.25 litres (5 cups) water

4 cm (1 1/2 inch) piece ginger, thinly sliced

155 g (1 bunch) asparagus, trimmed and cut into thirds

300 g (10 1/2 oz) silken tofu, cut into 2 cm (3/4 inch) cubes

2 tablespoons dried seaweed, shredded

1 Put the smoked fish, pickled ginger and wasabi on a plate. Cover with plastic wrap and refrigerate until required. Put the miso paste, stock, water and fresh ginger in a heavy-based pan. Bring slowly to the boil, stirring frequently, until the miso paste is dissolved.

2 Add the asparagus and tofu to the stock mixture. Cook for 2–3 minutes or until the asparagus is tender. Ladle the soup into bowls and top with seaweed. Serve immediately with the prepared salmon, ginger and wasabi.

Easy autumn entertaining

This seafood meal is so easy to prepare and delicious to eat, it's bound to be a family favourite for years to come. It can be served for lunch or dinner, and if it's a warm day, enjoy it outdoors and make the most of the lovely autumn sunshine.

Go for a simple and elegant table setting by dressing the dining table with lengths of inexpensive fabric – just trim the edges with pinking shears to stop it fraying.

MENU

Serve Fresh salmon cakes with dill frittata as a tasty appetizer. Spaghetti with chilli vongole makes a deliciously messy starter – remember the paper napkins. Creamy Prawns in tomato and fetta with garlic bread and salad make a tasty dish out of everyone's favourite seafood. Serve it with Tomato, zucchini and eggplant bake. Finish with coconut lemon tart and moreish Chocolate hazelnut brownies.

Get together with family and friends to celebrate life with a sumptuous seafood meal.

Choosing and storing shellfish

- Shellfish should have a fresh and pleasant – not overpowering – sea smell.
- Avoid shellfish with lots of open shells – they're not fresh.
- Live mussels, clams and pipis can be stored for one to three days in a damp hessian bag or in a bucket of water (fresh or salt) in a cool place. Don't refrigerate for long periods as this can kill them.
- It's best to buy and cook shellfish on the same day. If buying a few hours beforehand, wrap them in damp paper and place in the fridge; this keeps them fresh and alive. Don't bury them in ice; it will kill them. Store over ice with a layer of paper in between.
- If you have time, put vongole in a bowl of water with 1–2 tablespoons of flour or oatmeal; the vongole will eat it and empty of sand.

Fresh salmon cakes with dill frittata

Preparation time:

15 mins

Cooking time:

25 mins

SERVES 6

500 g (1 lb 2 oz) fresh salmon fillet, skin removed

2 slices white bread, chopped

1 small red onion, chopped

finely grated zest and juice of 1 lemon

salt and freshly ground black pepper

Frittata

1 desiree potato, thinly sliced

6 eggs

30 g (1 bunch) chives, chopped

salt and freshly ground black pepper

basil leaves, to serve

1   Preheat the oven to 180°C (350°F/Gas 4) and line a baking tray with baking paper. Roughly chop the salmon, then process it in a food processor until finely chopped (do not process to a paste). Transfer the salmon to a mixing bowl, then add the bread, onion, zest, juice and salt and pepper to taste. Mix until well combined.

2   Roll tablespoons of the mixture into balls. Place the balls on the prepared baking tray and bake in the oven for 12 minutes.

3   To make the frittata, line a 20 cm (8 inch) square tin with baking paper and layer the base with potato slices. Put the eggs, chives and salt and pepper in a bowl and whisk together. Pour the egg mixture over the potato. Bake for 10–12 minutes or until the egg is set and the potato is tender.

4   To serve, cut the frittata into small squares and top with a salmon cake. Sit a basil leaf on the top and secure with a toothpick pushed through to the frittata. Serve immediately.

Spaghetti with chilli vongole

Preparation time:

20 mins

Cooking time:

20 mins

SERVES 6

2 tablespoons olive oil

3 cloves garlic, finely chopped

2 small red chillies, seeds removed and finely chopped

2 small green chillies, seeds removed and finely
  chopped

125 ml (1/2 cup) white wine

125 ml (1/2 cup) stock

60 g (2 1/4 oz) butter, cubed

500 g (1 lb 2 oz) spaghetti

1 kg (2 lb 4 oz) baby clams (vongole), cleaned

chopped parsley

1 Heat the oil in a large, deep pan. Add the garlic and chillies and cook over a low heat for 2–3 minutes. Pour in the wine and stock, then bring slowly to the boil. Reduce to a simmer, then whisk in the butter and simmer, covered, for 6–7 minutes.

2 Cook the pasta in a pan of boiling water until tender. At the same time that you add the pasta to the pan, add the clams to the wine mixture, cover and cook for 4 minutes. Shake the pan to ensure the clams cook evenly. Remove any that are unopened.

3 Drain the pasta and place in a bowl. Add the clams, sauce and parsley. Toss together and serve immediately.

Prawns in tomato and fetta with garlic bread

Preparation time:

20 mins

Cooking time:

30 mins

SERVES 6

2 tablespoons olive oil

2 cloves garlic, finely chopped

1 onion, finely chopped

2 x 400 g (14 oz) cans chopped tomatoes

125 ml (1/2 cup) white wine

1 kg (2 lb 4 oz) raw prawns (shrimp)

200 g (7 oz) fetta cheese

5 g (1/4 bunch) thyme

Garlic bread

125 g (4 1/2 oz) butter, softened

3–4 cloves garlic, chopped

round loaf of bread or damper

1 Preheat the oven to 200°C (400°F/Gas 6). Lightly grease a shallow, rectangular ovenproof dish with a little of the oil.

2 Heat the rest of the oil in a large, heavy-based pan, add the garlic and onion, and cook over a medium heat until the onion is soft. Add the tomato and white wine, then stir until well combined. Bring slowly to the boil, then reduce to a simmer and cook for 10 minutes.

3 Peel and devein the prawns, then put them in the prepared dish. Pour the tomato sauce over them, then crumble the fetta and sprinkle it over the top.

4 Bake the prawns for about 10 minutes or until they change colour and the fetta starts to brown. Top with sprigs of thyme and serve with a wedge of garlic bread or crusty bread, if desired.

5 To make the garlic bread, mix the butter with garlic. Cut the bread into wedges and spread both sides of each wedge with butter. Wrap the loaf in foil and bake at 180°C (350°F/Gas 4) for 10 minutes. Serve hot with Fennel and walnut salad (page 219).

Fennel and walnut salad

Tomato, zucchini and eggplant bake

Fennel and walnut salad

Preparation time:

20 mins

Cooking time:

nil

SERVES 4

5 baby fennel, halved and sliced

100 g (3½ oz) walnuts, roughly chopped

juice of 2 oranges

sea salt flakes

freshly ground black pepper

shredded orange zest

Combine the fennel and walnuts in a large bowl. Pour the orange juice over the top and sprinkle with salt and pepper. Toss well. Top with orange zest and serve immediately.

Tomato, zucchini and eggplant bake

Preparation time:

10 mins

Cooking time:

30 mins

SERVES 4

2 small zucchini (courgettes), thinly sliced

3 Japanese eggplants (aubergines), thinly sliced

500 g (2 punnets) vine-ripened baby tomatoes

2 cloves garlic, finely chopped

60 ml (¼ cup) tarragon-vinegar

60 ml (¼ cup) olive oil

sea salt flakes

freshly ground black pepper

Preheat the oven to 200°C (400°F/Gas 6). Put the zucchini, eggplant, tomatoes and garlic in an ovenproof dish. Pour the vinegar and oil over the vegetables and stir to coat well. Sprinkle with salt and pepper. Bake for 25–30 minutes or until the vegetables are tender and the zucchini turns golden. Serve immediately.

Coconut lemon tart

Preparation time:

25 mins

Cooking time:

35 mins

SERVES 6

225 g (2 1/2 cups) desiccated coconut

145 g (2/3 cup) caster (superfine) sugar

60 g (1/2 cup) plain (all-purpose) flour

2 eggs, lightly beaten

395 g (14 oz) can sweetened condensed milk

extra 3 eggs

finely grated zest and juice of 3 lemons
   (about 185 ml/3/4 cup)

extra 115 g (1/2 cup) caster (superfine) sugar

1   Preheat the oven to 180°C (350°F/Gas 4). Lightly grease a 22 cm (9 inch) round, loose-bottomed, 3.5 cm (1 1/4 inch) deep, fluted flan tin and line the base with baking paper. Put the coconut, sugar and flour in a bowl and stir to combine. Make a well in the centre, add the eggs and stir to combine. Put the mixture into the base of the tin and, using your hands, press evenly over the base and up the sides. Bake for 20–25 minutes or until the edges are lightly browned. Stand on a wire rack to cool.

2   Pour the condensed milk into a medium-sized bowl. Separate the extra eggs, reserving the egg whites for topping. Add the egg yolks, lemon zest and juice to the condensed milk. Whisk until well combined. Pour the mixture into the pastry base and spread evenly.

3   Beat the egg whites until stiff peaks form. Slowly add the sugar, beating well after each addition until the meringue is thick and glossy. Spoon evenly over the filling. Bake for 5–10 minutes or until golden brown. Allow to cool for 5–10 minutes before removing from the tin. Serve warm or cold.

Chocolate hazelnut brownies

Preparation time:	
20 mins	

Cooking time:	
35 mins	

MAKES 24 SQUARES

80 ml (1/3 cup) black coffee

175 g (6 oz) butter, chopped

250 g (9 oz) dark chocolate, chopped

185 g (1 1/2 cups) plain (all-purpose) flour

60 g (1/2 cup) cocoa

330 g (1 1/2 cups) sugar

125 g (1 cup) roasted hazelnuts, roughly chopped

3 eggs, lightly beaten

extra 30 g (1/4 cup) sifted cocoa, for dusting

1 Add the coffee, butter and chocolate to a medium-sized saucepan. Stir over a low heat until the butter and chocolate are melted and the mixture becomes smooth. Preheat the oven to 180°C (350°F/Gas 4). Lightly grease a 30 x 20 cm (12 x 8 inch) baking tin. Line the base and long sides with baking paper.

2 Sift the flour and cocoa into a large mixing bowl. Add the sugar and nuts and stir to combine. Make a well in the centre, then pour in the chocolate mixture and eggs. Stir until the mixture is well combined and smooth.

3 Spoon the mixture into the prepared tin and bake for 35 minutes. Remove from the oven and stand on a wire rack to cool. Remove from the tin and when completely cool, cut into small squares and lightly dust with cocoa.

One-pan
roasts

Roasts have never been easier. With our foolproof method, you simply put the meat and vegies together in a pan and bake. You can enjoy this family favourite every night of the week and be sure that the family will gather round to share it. Serve your roast on individual plates that have been warmed or on a large platter.

Rules of the roast

The way a roast is handled after it is cooked determines its tenderness and juiciness. Always allow meat to rest for 15–20 minutes before carving. This simply means letting it stand so the fibres of the meat relax. Relaxed meat won't shrink and become tough to slice. To rest the roast, remove it from the oven, transfer to a heated plate or carving tray and cover with aluminium foil, to keep the meat warm.

Carving a roast

The aim of carving is to get the greatest number of slices that are attractive and tender.

Choose a knife that is comfortable to hold and of an adequate size. Keep the blade sharp and don't use your carving knife for any other purpose.

Remove any string and skewers as the meat is carved to prevent it from falling apart. Always carve across the grain – this means across the fibres of the muscle. The angle will vary slightly between each cut and type of meat. Apply just enough pressure to cut the fibres. Too much pressure will bruise or tear the meat. Carve with a slicing rather than a sawing motion, use the full length of the blade and follow through each slice.

Sauces, stocks and wines add flavour as well as moistness to the cooked roast.

Veal with fennel and pumpkin

Preparation time:

15 mins

Cooking time:

50 mins

COOK'S TIP

Veal nut is a lean cut with no bones. If you can't see the nut on display at the butcher, get them to cut one for you. A rolled breast of veal or small boned leg can be used in its place.

SERVES 4

30 g (1 bunch) sage, leaves only

8 thin slices prosciutto

750 g (1 lb 10 oz) veal nut (see Cook's tip)

4 small fennel, cut into quarters

750 g (1 lb 10 oz) pumpkin, cut into chunks

2 tablespoons olive oil

500 g (1 lb 2 oz) baby beans, tails removed

extra 2 teaspoons olive oil

70 g (½ cup) small black olives

1 Preheat the oven to 200°C (400°F/Gas 6). Lay the sage leaves on top of the veal, then arrange the prosciutto slices to cover them. Put the veal in a roasting tin and arrange the fennel and pumpkin around it. Drizzle with oil.

2 Cover the tin with a sheet of aluminium foil. Bake for 20 minutes, then remove the foil and bake for a further 25 minutes. Remove the veal, fennel and pumpkin from the roasting tin. Cover them with foil and sit in a warm place. Put the roasting tin on a medium heat on the stove and bring any juices to the boil, scraping the base of the dish to lift any sediment.

3 Wash the beans under cold running water, leaving the water clinging to the beans. Heat the extra oil in a medium, heavy-based pan. Add the beans and cook, tossing over a high heat for 1–2 minutes or until tender. Add the olives and toss together.

4 To serve, place the veal on a serving plate and spoon on the pan juices. Surround with the fennel and pumpkin. Put the beans in a serving bowl. Serve immediately.

Chicken with potato and leeks

Preparation time:

15 mins

Cooking time:

1 hour 5 mins

We used small chickens for this recipe. You can buy these in a twin-pack from the butcher or poultry shops. Don't use one large chicken as it will not be cooked in time.

SERVES 4

1.2 kg (2 lb 12 oz) desiree potatoes

2 leeks

90 g (3¼ oz) butter, softened

1 handful tarragon, roughly chopped

salt and freshly ground black pepper

2 x 1 kg (2 lb 4 oz) chickens (see Cook's tip)

250 ml (1 cup) chicken stock

extra sprigs of tarragon, to garnish

steamed brussels sprouts or sugar snap peas,

   for serving

1 Preheat the oven to 200°C (400°F/Gas 6). Cut the potatoes and leeks into 1 cm (½ inch) thick slices. Place in a roasting tin. Put the softened butter, tarragon, salt and pepper in a small bowl. Beat with a wooden spoon until well combined.

2 Using your thumb, loosen the skin from each chicken breast, being careful not to tear it. Smear one-half of the butter mixture on each breast. Pull over the skin and pat to even out the butter. Tie the legs of each chicken together with string, then sit the chickens on top of the potatoes and leeks. Pour the stock over the chickens, potatoes and leeks. Cover with a sheet of baking paper and then a sheet of aluminium foil.

3 Cook for 30 minutes. Remove from the oven, then remove the paper and foil. Return to the oven and cook for a further 35 minutes or until the potatoes are tender. Transfer the chickens, potatoes and leeks to a warmed plate. Top with tarragon. Serve with brussels sprouts or sugar snap peas, if desired.

Pork with maple syrup and star anise

Preparation time:

15 mins

Cooking time:

1 hour 10 mins

SERVES 4

1 teaspoon sesame oil

8 cm (3 inch) piece ginger, finely chopped

250 ml (1 cup) maple syrup

60 ml (¼ cup) brown vinegar

6 star anise

6 long, thin sweet potatoes

2 bunches bulb spring onions

1.25 kg (2 lb 12 oz) rolled forequarter pork
   (see Cook's tip)

1 teaspoon sea salt flakes

375 g (1 bunch) baby bok choy (pak choi),
   cut in half lengthways

1 Preheat the oven to 200°C (400°F/Gas 6). Heat the sesame oil in a small pan, add the ginger and cook for 1 minute. Add the maple syrup, brown vinegar and star anise and boil for 2 minutes. Reduce to a simmer and cook for 2 more minutes.

2 Peel the sweet potatoes and cut each into three pieces. Trim the long, green end from each spring onion. Sit the pork in the baking dish and sprinkle with salt. Arrange the sweet potatoes and spring onions around the pork. Pour the maple-syrup mixture only over sweet potato and onions – not the pork. Cover with foil. Bake, covered, for 30 minutes. Remove the foil and bake for a further 35 minutes.

3 Remove the pork, potatoes and onions. Cover with foil and stand in a warm place. Place the baking dish on a medium heat on the stove and cook until the mixture is reduced by half. Put the bok choy in a pan, add a spoonful of water and cook on high, tossing, until it turns bright green.

4 Cut the pork into thin slices. Place on a warm plate. Spoon the pan juices over the pork. Serve with sweet potato, spring onions and the bok choy.

Lamb with lemon and bean purée and spinach salad

Preparation time:

30 mins

Cooking time:

1 hour 15 mins

COOK'S TIP

We've used an Easy Carve leg of lamb which has had the large bone removed and the small shank bone left intact. A small, tunnel-boned leg of lamb can be used in its place.

SERVES 6

shredded zest of 1 lemon

3 cloves garlic, chopped

25 g (1 bunch) oregano, chopped

1 Easy Carve leg of lamb (see Cook's tip)

8 large desiree potatoes, cut into wedges

3 lemons, 2 cut into wedges, the third juiced

2 tablespoons honey

sea salt flakes

Bean purée

2 tablespoons olive oil

2 cloves garlic

2 x 400 g (14 oz) cans cannellini (white) beans, well drained

juice of 1 small lemon

salt and freshly ground black pepper

Spinach salad

100 g (3 handfuls) baby English spinach leaves, washed and patted dry

100 g (3 1/2 oz) pine nuts, toasted

a little olive oil and white-wine vinegar

1 Preheat the oven to 200°C (400°F/Gas 6). Combine the lemon zest, garlic and oregano, then stuff the lamb with it. Put the lamb in a large roasting tin. Arrange the potato and lemon wedges around the outside of the lamb. Put the lemon juice and honey in a small bowl and stir well, then pour over the lamb and potatoes. Sprinkle with sea salt. Cover the dish with aluminium foil. Bake for 30 minutes, then remove the foil and cook for a further 40–45 minutes. Remove the lamb from the dish, cover with foil and stand for 10 minutes before cutting into thin slices. Serve with the Bean purée and Spinach salad.

2 To make the Bean purée, heat the oil in a small pan, add the garlic and cook until golden. Remove from the heat. Put the oil, garlic, beans, lemon juice and salt and pepper in a food processor and process until smooth. Serve immediately.

3 Put the spinach in a large bowl with the pine nuts, oil and vinegar. Toss well.

Beef with redcurrant jelly and red wine

Preparation time:

15 mins

Cooking time:

1 hour 10 mins

COOK'S TIP

A whole piece of rump has been used for this recipe. It has a good layer of fat on top which will add to the flavour and tenderness of the beef. You can trim off a little of the fat, if you prefer. A sirloin of topside roast can be used in its place.

SERVES 4

1 tablespoon olive oil

2 cloves garlic, thinly sliced

250 ml (1 cup) redcurrant jelly

250 ml (1 cup) red wine

6 beetroot, trimmed

4 parsnips

1.25 kg (2 lb 12 oz) rump (for roasting) (see Cook's tip)

310 g (2 bunches) asparagus, trimmed

extra 2 teaspoons olive oil

salt and freshly ground black pepper

1 Preheat the oven to 200°C (400°F/Gas 6). Heat the oil in a small pan, add the garlic and cook for 1–2 minutes. Add the jelly and red wine. Stir over a medium heat until the jelly is dissolved. Bring slowly to the boil, then reduce to a simmer and cook for a further 3–4 minutes.

2 Wash the beetroot and parsnips, but do not peel them. Cut the beetroot into quarters and the parsnips into large chunks. Sit the beef in a roasting tin, then arrange the beetroot and parsnips around the beef. Pour over the redcurrant mixture. Cover with foil and cook for 30 minutes. Remove the foil and roast until the beetroot is tender.

3 Remove the beef and vegetables from the tin and stand covered with foil in a warm area. Put the tin over a medium heat on the stove and bring the pan juices to the boil, then cook for 2–3 minutes. Pour into a jug. Cut the beef into thin slices.

4 Wash the asparagus. Heat the extra oil in a wide pan, add the asparagus and cook, tossing for 1–2 minutes or until the asparagus becomes tender. Season with salt and pepper. Serve the beef with the vegetables and spoon the sauce over the meat.

apples and pears

There can be little wonder that Eve succumbed to the temptation of biting into a crisp, crunchy apple. This fruit has a delightfully sweet flavour right down to the last bite. Eve would have found it hard to say no to a juicy pear, too. They're equally as delicious and just as versatile in cooking.

Make your own apple sauce

To make apple sauce, peel, quarter and core 3 large green apples. Put in a saucepan and cover with cold water. Bring slowly to the boil. Reduce to a simmer and cook until the apples are soft and the liquid has evaporated. Stir with a fork during cooking to break up the apples. Season to taste with salt, pepper and a little sugar. Serve with your favourite pork dish.

Choosing and storing pears

A ripe pear has a strong, fresh, sweet aroma and should give a little when pressed gently at the stem. It's best to buy pears when they're slightly green, then let them ripen at room temperature. You can speed up the ripening process by putting them in a brown paper bag with an apple. Pears bruise easily so don't stack them in a fruit bowl. Store ripe pears in a single layer in the vegetable crisper of your refrigerator.

Choosing and storing apples

There's a wide variety of apples available at this time of year – and each has a different look, taste and texture.

Apples should be firm to the touch with unblemished skin, an even colour and a sweet aroma. The best flavour comes from those varieties in peak season, which are also usually the cheapest to buy.

Many apples have a wax coating to make them look shiny. Avoid these, as it's hard to see how ripe they are.

For short storage, keep apples in a fruit bowl in a cool place. For longer storage, put them in a plastic bag in the vegetable crisper.

Pears are not only delicious, they're also incredibly healthy and an excellent source of dietary fibre.

Potato rosti with ham steaks

Preparation time:

10 mins

Cooking time:

10 mins

SERVES 4

500 g (1 lb 2 oz) sebago (white-skinned) potatoes,
  peeled and grated

2 tablespoons finely chopped chives

salt and freshly ground black pepper

8 very thick slices of ham, off the bone

1 tablespoon olive oil

Combine the grated potato and chopped chives in a large bowl. Season well with salt and pepper. Put the ham onto a baking tray and place under a hot grill (broiler). Cook for 4–5 minutes or until the steaks are heated through and beginning to colour. Heat the oil in a medium-sized, non-stick frypan over a medium heat. Drop 40 g (1/4 cup) measures of the potato mixture into the pan and flatten slightly with a spatula. Cook for 2 minutes on each side until the potato rosti are crisp, brown and cooked through. Serve immediately with the ham steaks and Pickled pears.

Pickled pears

Preparation time:

15 mins

Cooking time:

1 1/2 hours

COOK'S TIP

Pickled pears can be stored in
the fridge for up to 4 weeks.

MAKES 2 CUPS

250 ml (1 cup) red wine

250 ml (1 cup) red-wine vinegar

220 g (1 cup) white sugar

90 g (1/4 cup) honey

1 tablespoon black peppercorns

1 teaspoon whole cloves

2 bay leaves

1 large cinnamon stick

a few strips of lemon zest

1 kg (2 lb 4 oz) small Packham pears, quartered

Put everything except the pears in a pan. Cook on a low heat, stirring, until the sugar dissolves. Bring slowly to the boil. Reduce to a simmer and cook for 5 minutes. Add the pears to the wine syrup. Cook on a low heat for 45 minutes or until the pears are tender and pinkish in colour. Remove the pears with a slotted spoon and put into a hot, sterilized jar. Boil the syrup rapidly until it is reduced by half and slightly thickened. Pour the hot syrup into the jar, making sure the pears are covered, then seal the jar. Serve the pickled pears as an accompaniment to Potato rosti with ham steaks.

Five-spice pork and apples

Preparation time:

20 mins

Cooking time:

55 mins

COOK'S TIP

Kecap manis is an Indonesian sweet soy sauce. It is available from supermarkets. If you can't find it, mix a little brown sugar into ordinary soy sauce.

SERVES 6

6 Pink Lady apples

splash of lemon juice

3 pork fillets (about 1 kg)

2 tablespoons peanut oil

1 tablespoon five-spice powder

5 cm (2 inch) piece ginger, chopped

2 cloves garlic, chopped

4 spring onions (scallions), chopped

2 tablespoons dark brown sugar

125 ml (½ cup) kecap manis (see Cook's tip)

60 ml (¼ cup) dry sherry

2 tablespoons apple-cider vinegar

To serve

steamed rice noodles

steamed Chinese greens

2 spring onions (scallions), chopped

1　Cut the apples into quarters and remove the cores. Place the apples in a large bowl of water with a squeeze of lemon to stop them turning brown. Trim the fat and sinew from the pork and cut into 5 cm (2 inch) pieces.

2　Drain the apples and pat dry with a paper towel. Heat the oil in a large, heavy-based pan, add the apples in a single layer and cook on a medium heat until lightly browned all over. Remove and set aside.

3　Add the meat to the pan in three batches and cook on a medium heat until browned. Remove and put in a clay pot or a deep, heavy-based saucepan with a lid.

4　Add the five-spice powder, ginger, garlic and spring onion to the empty pan and cook, stirring, for about 1 minute. Add the brown sugar, kecap manis, sherry and vinegar and stir to combine. Bring to the boil, then reduce to a simmer. Cook for 1 minute. Pour the sauce over the pork and mix well. Put the lid on the pan and cook over a medium heat for 20 minutes. Remove the lid, place the apples on top and cook for 10–15 minutes or until the apples are tender. Stir well. Serve with noodles and Chinese greens and top with spring onion.

Pear and brie tart

Preparation time:

30 mins plus refrigeration
and cooling

Cooking time:

1 hour 35 mins

SERVES 8

250 g (2 cups) plain (all-purpose) flour

1 teaspoon baking powder

125 g (4½ oz) butter, chilled and chopped

60 g (½ cup) walnuts, finely chopped

4–5 tablespoons cold water

300 g (10½ oz) fresh ricotta cheese

400 g (14 oz) brie cheese, finely chopped

1 egg

2 large firm green pears

80 g (¼ cup) lime marmalade

1 Preheat the oven to 200°C (400°F/Gas 6). Lightly grease a 22 cm (9 inch) loose-bottomed flan tin. Put the flour, baking powder and butter in a food processor. Process for 30 seconds. Add the chopped walnuts and process again. Pour the water in slowly, until the mixture comes together.

2 Turn the mixture onto a lightly floured surface, knead until smooth, then roll into a ball. Press the ball flat and wrap in plastic wrap. Refrigerate for 30 minutes.

3 Roll out the pastry between two sheets of baking paper or plastic wrap until it is large enough to fit into the flan tin. Remove the paper and ease the pastry into the tin, taking care not to stretch it. Carefully trim the excess pastry with a large, sharp knife.

4 Cover the pastry with a piece of baking paper large enough to come up the sides of the tin. Spread a layer of dried beans or rice evenly over the paper. Put on a baking tray and bake for 20 minutes. Remove the tin from the oven and carefully remove the paper and beans or rice. Return the pastry in the tin to the oven for a further 10 minutes. Cool completely.

5 Reduce the oven temperature to 180°C (350°F/Gas 4). Put the ricotta, brie and egg in a medium-sized bowl. Stir until well combined and then spoon into the pastry shell. Cut the pears into quarters, then cut each quarter into slices. Lay the slices around the top of the tart, overlapping each one slightly. Brush with lime marmalade and bake for 50–60 minutes or until the filling is set and the pears are golden and tender.

Apple and pear wafers

Preparation time:

20 mins

Cooking time:

35 mins

COOK'S TIP

These sweet crispy wafers are a moreish treat at any time of the day. The kids will also love them in their lunch boxes.

SERVES 6

1 red or green apple

1 pear

splash of lemon juice

500 ml (2 cups) water

220 g (1 cup) sugar

1 Cut each apple and pear into paper-thin slices and put in a bowl of water with lemon juice to stop them from going brown. Put the water and sugar in a pan. Stir over a low heat until the sugar has dissolved and the mixture comes to the boil.

2 Drain the apple and pear slices and drop one at a time into the sugar syrup. Reduce the heat and simmer for 8 minutes or until the fruit is transparent. Allow the fruit to cool in the syrup.

3 Preheat the oven to 160°C (310°F/Gas 2). Remove the fruit from the syrup with tongs and dry on paper towel. Place on baking trays lined with baking paper. Bake for 20–25 minutes or until crisp. Remove from the oven and allow to cool on a tray before removing. Store in an airtight container.

Apple teacake

Preparation time:

20 mins

Cooking time:

55 mins

This teacake is best eaten on the day of baking. It can be served warm as a dessert with lashings of custard or cream.

MAKES A 20 CM (8 INCH) ROUND CAKE

2 medium red apples

125 g (4½ oz) butter

115 g (½ cup) caster (superfine) sugar

2 eggs, lightly beaten

250 g (2 cups) self-raising flour

125 ml (½ cup) milk

extra 30 g (1 oz) butter, melted

extra 1 tablespoon caster (superfine) sugar

1 Preheat the oven to 180°C (350°F/Gas 4). Lightly grease a 20 cm (8 inch) round springform tin and line the base with baking paper.

2 Core and quarter each apple. Using a sharp knife, cut each quarter into very thin slices. Cover with cold water. Combine the butter and sugar in a bowl and beat with electric beaters until creamy. Add the eggs and beat thoroughly.

3 Using a large metal spoon, fold the flour and milk into the butter mixture until just combined. Spoon the mixture into the prepared tin and smooth the surface.

4 Arrange the drained apple, slightly overlapping, on top of the cake. Bake for 55–60 minutes or until a skewer comes out clean when inserted in the centre. Remove from the oven and stand on a wire rack to cool slightly. Release from the tin, then brush the top with melted butter and sprinkle with sugar. Serve warm.

buttermilk

Buttermilk is deliciously rich and tasty and, even better, it's low in fat. So next time you're shopping, reach for this creamy, versatile milk and butter up the whole family. Traditionally, buttermilk was the liquid that drained from the churn as the butter was made. But today, buttermilk is made from skim milk and special bacterial cultures. It has a similar flavour to plain yoghurt and a delightfully rich texture.

The lower fat milk

Buttermilk has the same food value as non-fat milk. And because buttermilk is produced from skim milk, it also has a similar nutritional value. Weight watchers rejoice! Not only is buttermilk practically fat-free, but it also has only half the kilojoules of fresh milk. All this and more, as it also contains complete protein and B-group vitamins, in particular riboflavin and calcium.

Buttermilk in cooking

- Because of its high acid content, buttermilk has a tenderizing effect on flour so it makes cakes, scones and breads even more soft and luscious.
- Buttermilk is very easily digested by the stomach so it's fantastic in milk puddings and drinks.
- Add a little buttermilk to your mashed potatoes for loads of flavour minus the fat of traditional mash.

Buying and storing buttermilk

You don't have to go out of your way to find buttermilk. You can buy it in the dairy section of most supermarkets and anywhere milk is sold.

You can store an unopened carton of buttermilk in the refrigerator for up to 15 days. After opening, buttermilk should be used within a week because the acidity will continue to develop, eventually causing an unpleasant bitter taste.

This thick, creamy milk is low in fat and full of goodness. Add it to your shopping list and open up a new world of flavours.

Pork simmered in buttermilk

Preparation time:

10 mins

Cooking time:

1 hour 35 mins

SERVES 6

30 g (1 oz) butter

1 tablespoon olive oil

2 kg (4 lb 8 oz) piece pork scotch fillet

freshly ground black pepper

3 cloves garlic, finely chopped

600 ml (21 fl oz) buttermilk

extra 1 tablespoon olive oil

1 kg (2 bunches) English spinach, washed and trimmed

60 g (½ cup) raisins

1   Heat the butter and oil in a large, heavy-based pan. Season the pork with the pepper and brown well, on a medium heat. Add the garlic and half the buttermilk to the pan, bring slowly to the boil and reduce to a very low simmer. Cover with a tight-fitting lid and cook for 1 hour.

2   After the hour, the milk will have reduced, thickened and turned a pale golden brown. Add the remaining milk and cook, covered, for another 35 minutes. Remove the pork from the pan, cover with aluminium foil and stand for 10 minutes.

3   Return the pan to the heat and bring the buttermilk mixture to the boil. Reduce to a simmer and cook for 3–4 minutes. The mixture will separate and have small clumps of solids. Pour this through a fine strainer.

4   Heat the extra oil in a medium, heavy-based pan. Add the spinach and raisins and cook, stirring until the spinach just starts to wilt. Place the spinach on a warm serving plate. Cut the meat into thin slices and lay it over the spinach. Spoon a little of the strained clear liquid from the pan over the meat. Serve immediately.

Lime spice syrup cake

Preparation time:

20 mins

Cooking time:

1 hour

COOK'S TIP

We've topped our cake with
softened figs. If you'd like to
do the same, cut 6 fresh figs
into quarters, but don't cut all
the way through (they should
remain intact.) Sprinkle with
1 tablespoon demerara sugar.
Cook under a preheated grill
(broiler) until the sugar starts
to melt.

SERVES 6

185 g (6½ oz) unsalted butter, chopped

230 g (1 cup) caster (superfine) sugar

grated zest and juice from 2 limes

4 eggs, separated

250 g (2 cups) plain (all-purpose) flour

1 tablespoon ground cinnamon

1 tablespoon ground nutmeg

2 teaspoons ground cardamom

1 teaspoon baking powder

1 teaspoon bicarbonate of soda

250 ml (1 cup) buttermilk

For the syrup

125 ml (½ cup) water

165 g (¾ cup) sugar

juice of 2 limes

strip of lime zest

1 cinnamon stick

4 cardamom pods, bruised

1   Preheat the oven to 180°C (350°F/Gas 4). Brush a 23 cm (9 inch) round tin with melted butter and line the base with baking paper. Put the butter, sugar and lime zest in a small bowl and beat until light and creamy. Add the egg yolks one at a time, beating well after each addition. Transfer to a large mixing bowl. Sift together the flour, spices, baking powder and bicarbonate of soda. Fold into the butter mixture alternately with the buttermilk and lime juice.

2   Beat the egg whites in a clean dry bowl until soft peaks form. Fold into the batter with a large metal spoon until just combined. Spoon into the prepared tin. Bake for 55–60 minutes or until a skewer inserted in the centre of the cake comes out clean. Cool for 5 minutes before turning out onto a wire rack.

3   To make the syrup, put the water, sugar and lime juice in a medium-sized, heavy-based pan. Stir over a low heat until the sugar is dissolved. Add the lime zest, cinnamon stick and cardamom pods. Bring to the boil and then simmer for 5 minutes. Keep the cake on its wire rack and place over a tray. Pour hot syrup onto the cake through a sieve. Transfer to a serving plate and serve with grilled sugared figs and softly whipped cream or mascarpone on the side.

Buttermilk puddings

Preparation time:

10 mins plus
several hours chilling

Cooking time:

5 mins

COOK'S TIP

Sprinkle a few drops of cold
water on the plate you're going to
serve the pudding on. That way,
if the pudding isn't centred on
the plate, it's easy to slide it over.

SERVES 6

600 ml (21 fl oz) buttermilk

165 g (3/4 cup) sugar

6 cardamom pods, bruised

1 strip orange zest

1 tablespoon gelatine

125 ml (1/2 cup) hot water

4 small oranges, peeled and sliced

1 tablespoon sugar

1   Place the buttermilk, sugar, cardamom pods and orange zest in a small
    pan and stir over a low heat until the sugar dissolves. Do not boil. Stand for
    10 minutes to allow the flavours to infuse. Pour through a strainer into a jug.

2   Put hot water into a small bowl, sprinkle the gelatine over it and whisk with a
    fork to dissolve the gelatine. Pour gelatine into the infused milk and stir to
    combine. Divide the mixture evenly among six 125 ml (1/2 cup) wetted moulds.
    Place the moulds on a tray and refrigerate for several hours or until set.

3   Just before serving, turn the chilled puddings out onto a plate. Place the
    orange slices on a baking tray that's been lined with foil. Sprinkle with sugar
    and cook under a preheated hot grill (broiler) until the sugar starts to brown.
    Serve the buttermilk puddings with a couple of the cooked orange slices on
    the side.

Strawberry smoothie

Preparation time:

5 mins

MAKES 1 SMOOTHIE

250 ml (1 cup) buttermilk

1 tablespoon honey

handful of chopped strawberries or raspberries

3–4 ice cubes

Blend the buttermilk, honey, strawberries or raspberries and ice cubes in a blender until smooth. Drink immediately.

Mint cooler

Preparation time:

5 mins

MAKES 1 SMOOTHIE

250 ml (1 cup) buttermilk

10 g (½ cup) mint leaves

3–4 ice cubes

extra mint leaves

Blend the buttermilk, mint leaves and a ice cubes in a blender until the mint is finely chopped. Garnish with mint leaves and drink immediately.

All about
honey

No wonder honey was celebrated as the food of the gods in ancient times, it was the first sweetener known to humankind. Considered a miracle food, it was used to preserve fruits, nuts and edible flowers, which were the ingredients for the sought-after delicacy sweetmeat.

Honey also gave rise to one of the world's first intoxicating drinks – mead. This was made by mixing honey with water and letting it ferment.

Choosing and buying honey

Honeys range in colour from light and clear, to thick and opaque, and each offers a distinct flavour, depending on the flower from which the honey was harvested.

With the enormous variety of honey that is available from supermarkets, delicatessens and health food stores, it can be difficult to choose a honey that suits you. A general rule of thumb is the darker the honey, the stronger the flavour. Any type of honey may be used in our recipes.

Baklava

Baklava is one of the most well known recipes featuring honey. It is a traditional Greek sweet packed with nuts and drenched in a thick honey syrup. Baklava is best made the day before serving so the syrup can soak through the layers of pastry and make the baklava gloriously moist and rich.

Storing and cooking with honey

Honey is best kept in a cool, dry place, well away from light and never in your refrigerator. Over time, it will crystallize, becoming cloudier, thicker and more grainy in texture, until eventually it sets hard. However, there is nothing wrong with the honey when it crystallizes and you can still eat it. To liquefy the honey, simply sit the jar in hot water and leave for 20 minutes or so.

Honey tastes wonderful in both sweet and savoury dishes. When measuring honey, wet your cup or spoon first so the honey slides out easily.

Need a soother for a sore throat?
A spoonful of your favourite
honey will work wonders.

Baked pork spare ribs with honey glaze

Preparation time:

15 mins

Cooking time:

30 mins

COOK'S TIP

We've baked the ribs in the oven; if you prefer, you can barbecue them and they'll take about the same amount of time.

SERVES 4

1 kg (2 lb 4 oz) lean pork spare ribs

1 teaspoon freshly ground black pepper

2 cloves garlic, finely chopped

1 tablespoon ground cardamom

1 tablespoon ground cumin

1/2 teaspoon sea salt flakes

175 g (1/2 cup) honey

zest and juice of 2 limes

1 teaspoon cardamom seeds

85 g (1/2 bunch) spring onions (scallions), trimmed

1 Preheat the oven to 200°C (400°F/Gas 6). Place the spare ribs in a medium-sized heavy-based pan, then cover with cold water and add the pepper. Bring slowly to the boil, then reduce to a simmer, cover and cook for 10 minutes.

2 Put the garlic, cardamom, cumin and sea salt flakes in a small bowl and mix until combined. Drain the pork ribs and place them on a baking tray in a single layer. Coat both sides of each rib with an equal amount of the garlic mixture. Set aside.

3 Put the honey, lime zest, juice and cardamom seeds in a small pan and stir over a low heat for 3–4 minutes. Bring the mixture to the boil, and boil for 1 minute. Spoon half of the honey glaze over the spare ribs. Bake for 10 minutes, turn the ribs, then spoon over the remaining glaze. Bake for a further 10 minutes. Serve topped with spring onions.

Crispy chicken with honey lemon sauce

Preparation time:	SERVES 4
20 mins	4 single chicken breasts
	2 egg whites
Cooking time:	2 tablespoons soy sauce
25 mins	125 g (1 cup) cornflour (cornstarch)
	splash of olive oil
	175 g (½ cup) honey
	125 ml (½ cup) chicken stock
	juice of 1 lemon
	5 cm (2 inch) piece ginger, cut into thin shreds
	extra 2 teaspoons cornflour (cornstarch)
	1 tablespoon dry sherry
	steamed Chinese greens, for serving

1 Preheat the oven to 200°C (400°F/Gas 6). Line a baking tray with baking paper. Remove any sinew and excess fat from the chicken. Cut each breast into 3–4 slices, cutting on an angle across the width of the breast.

2 Put the egg whites and soy sauce in a bowl and whisk until the mixture starts to foam. Put the cornflour in a large thick plastic bag. Dip the chicken into the egg white mixture, then put in the bag containing the cornflour. Secure the top of the bag and shake to coat the chicken pieces.

3 Place the chicken pieces on the prepared tray and sprinkle with a little olive oil. Bake for 10–15 minutes or until the chicken pieces are cooked through and crispy. Put the honey, chicken stock, lemon juice and ginger in a small heavy-based pan. Stir to combine, bring slowly to the boil, then reduce to a simmer. Simmer for 3–4 minutes.

4 Blend the extra cornflour with the sherry, then add it to the honey mixture and stir continuously until the mixture comes to the boil. Reduce to a simmer and simmer for 3–4 minutes. Serve the chicken with steamed Chinese greens and spoon some of the sauce over the top.

Baklava

Preparation time:

20 mins

Cooking time:

30 mins

MAKES 24 SQUARES

350 g (1 cup) honey

125 ml (½ cup) water

1 cinnamon stick

1 strip lemon zest

4 whole cloves

375 g (13 oz) almonds

150 g (5½ oz) walnut halves

2 teaspoons ground cinnamon

2 teaspoons mixed spice

1 tablespoon sugar

2 tablespoon olive oil

16 sheets filo pastry

1 Put the honey, water, cinnamon stick, lemon zest and cloves in a medium-sized, heavy-based pan and stir to combine. Bring slowly to the boil, then reduce to a simmer and cook for 8–10 minutes. Set aside to cool.

2 Preheat the oven to 180°C (350°F/Gas 4). Put the almonds, walnut halves, ground cinnamon, mixed spice and sugar in a food processor and process until the nuts are finely chopped.

3 Brush the base of a 28 x 18 cm (11 x 7 inch) tin with olive oil. Brush a sheet of filo pastry with olive oil, then fold in half widthways and place in the tin. Repeat this process with another three sheets of filo pastry. Spread one-third of the processed nut mixture evenly over the filo pastry.

4 Repeat the process using four sheets of pastry at a time, with the nut mixture layered in between. When the final four sheets of pastry are on top, tuck in any overhanging pastry from the sides and brush the top with olive oil. Use a large, sharp knife to score the baklava into quarters lengthways. (Do not cut through the base.)

5 Bake for 30 minutes, then pour the cooled syrup over the hot baklava. Leave to cool. Cut baklava into squares before serving.

Honey cake

Preparation time:

20 mins

Cooking time:

1 hour

MAKES A 23 CM (9 INCH) ROUND CAKE

185 g (1 1/2 cups) plain (all-purpose) flour

125 g (1 cup) self-raising flour

1/2 teaspoon bicarbonate of soda

125 g (2/3 cup) dark brown sugar

250 g (9 oz) butter, melted

350 g (1 cup) honey

185 ml (3/4 cup) milk

1 tablespoon vanilla essence

sifted icing (confectioners') sugar, for dusting

1   Preheat the oven to 160°C (310°F/Gas 2). Lightly grease a deep 23 cm (9 inch) round tin. Line the base and sides with baking paper.

2   Sift the flours and bicarbonate of soda into a large bowl. Add the sugar and stir well. Add the butter, honey, milk and vanilla essence. Beat on low speed with an electric beater for 1–2 minutes or until well combined. Increase to a high speed and beat for 3–4 minutes or until the mixture becomes thicker and lighter in colour.

3   Spoon the mixture into the prepared tin and smooth the top. Bake for 1 hour or until a skewer comes out clean when inserted into the centre of the cake. Stand on a wire rack to cool for 10 minutes before turning out. Dust the cake with icing sugar just before serving.

Honey and almond slice

Preparation time:

25 mins plus

20 mins chilling

Cooking time:

45 mins

SERVES 8

100 g (3½ oz) whole blanched almonds, toasted

155 g (1¼ cups) plain (all-purpose) flour

½ teaspoon baking powder

2 teaspoons ground ginger

100 g (3½ oz) butter, chilled, cubed

2 tablespoons honey

1 tablespoon chilled water

Topping

100 g (3½ oz) butter

260 g (¾ cup) honey

55 g (¼ cup) soft brown sugar

1 teaspoon vanilla essence

80 ml (⅓ cup) cream

1 egg, lightly beaten

200 g (7 oz) flaked almonds

1 Preheat the oven to 180°C (350°F/Gas 4). Line the base of a 28 x 18 cm (11 x 7 inch) tin with baking paper. Finely chop the whole almonds in a food processor.

2 Add the flour, baking powder and ginger to the almonds and process to combine. Add the butter and process until the mixture resembles fine breadcrumbs. Add the honey and water and blend until the pastry just comes together to form a ball.

3 Press the pastry into the prepared tin with the back of a large metal spoon or your fingertips. Prick the base with a fork. Bake for 12 minutes or until light golden. Cool on a wire rack.

4 To make the topping, put the butter, honey, brown sugar and vanilla in a medium-sized, heavy-based saucepan. Stir to combine. Bring slowly to the boil, stirring occasionally, and cook for 3–4 minutes. Remove from the heat, then stir in the cream. Pour the mixture into a heatproof bowl and chill in the fridge for 20 minutes or until cool and thick. Stir in the egg and flaked almonds. Spread the almond mixture evenly over the slice base. Reduce the oven temperature to 170°C (325°F/Gas 3) and bake for a further 30–35 minutes or until golden and firm to the touch. Set aside to cool to room temperature. Serve cut into squares.

Olive oil cakes

Making cakes with olive oil is so simple – no creaming, melting or rubbing. Just measure, pour, stir briefly and pop the tin into the oven. So strike it rich with one of the deliciously moist and easy-to-bake cakes on the following pages.

Choosing your oil

There's a wide range of olive oils available in supermarkets today, from fruity extra virgin to extra light. You'll find each kind varies in colour and flavour, and although all are suitable to use in these recipes, it's best to combine the more robust oils in the strongly flavoured cakes such as gingerbread and the more delicate, lighter-tasting oils in plainer cakes such as the Orange and almond cake.

The good oil

Not only is olive oil tasty and versatile, it's also good for you, being high in monounsaturated fats and containing myriad antioxidants. These substances may help protect against cardiovascular disease and certain cancers. When substituted for saturated fats, they may also reduce the risk of developing diabetes. So enjoy a slice of cake as an occasional treat and don't feel guilty about it – it's good for your health!

Polenta and caraway seed cake

This aromatic cake cuts well and has a strong flavour. Serve it with a wedge of Cheddar for a savoury snack, or topped with fig jam if you're in the mood for something sweet.

Line the base of your tin with baking paper so the cake can be easily removed.

Orange and almond cake

Preparation time:

20 mins

Cooking time:

1 hour

MAKES A 20 CM (8 INCH) SQUARE CAKE

185 g (1½ cups) plain (all-purpose) flour, sifted

2 teaspoons baking powder, sifted

100 g (3½ oz) ground almonds

170 g (¾ cup) caster (superfine) sugar

3 eggs, lightly beaten

125 ml (½ cup) olive oil

finely grated zest and juice of 2 oranges

100 g (3½ oz) whole blanched almonds

1 Preheat the oven to 180°C (350°F/Gas 4). Lightly grease a deep 20 cm (8 inch) square tin and line the base with baking paper. Put the flour, baking powder, almonds and sugar into the bowl of a large food processor. Process for 30 seconds or until just combined.

2 Add the eggs, olive oil, orange zest and juice to the processor and process until the mixture is just combined and smooth. Spoon into the prepared cake tin and smooth the surface. Decorate with almonds. Bake for 55–60 minutes or until the cake is well risen and firm and a skewer inserted in the centre comes out clean. Remove from the oven and stand on a wire rack for 10 minutes before turning out.

Polenta and caraway seed cake

Preparation time:

15 mins

Cooking time:

50 mins

MAKES A 20 CM (8 INCH) ROUND CAKE

185 g (1½ cups) self-raising flour

150 g (1 cup) polenta

1 tablespoon caraway seeds

125 ml (½ cup) olive oil

55 g (¼ cup) caster (superfine) sugar

2 eggs, lightly beaten

125 ml (½ cup) milk

extra caraway seeds

Cheddar cheese, for serving, optional

1 Preheat the oven to 180°C (350°F/Gas 4). Lightly grease a deep 20 cm (8 inch) round tin and line the base and sides with baking paper. Sift the flour into a medium-sized bowl, then add the polenta and caraway seeds. Stir until well combined.

2 Put the olive oil and caster sugar into a small bowl and beat until light and fluffy. Add the eggs a little at a time, beating well after each addition. Make a well in the centre of the polenta mixture and add the oil mixture. Slowly pour in the milk and stir with a large metal spoon until well combined.

3 Spoon the batter into the prepared cake tin and bake for 45–50 minutes or until the cake is cooked through and a skewer inserted into the centre comes out clean. Place on a wire rack and allow to cool for 5 minutes before removing from the tin. Serve the cake savoury style with a wedge of Cheddar, or topped with fig jam for a sweet treat, if desired.

Apricot and banana cake

Preparation time:
30 mins plus
40 mins standing

Cooking time:
1 1/2 hours

MAKES A 23 CM (9 INCH) ROUND CAKE

200 g (1 cup) dried apricots, roughly chopped

125 ml (1/2 cup) orange juice

250 g (2 cups) plain (all-purpose) flour

1 1/2 teaspoons bicarbonate of soda

2 teaspoons ground cinnamon

1 teaspoon ground nutmeg

460 g (2 cups) caster (superfine) sugar

250 ml (1 cup) olive oil

1 tablespoon vanilla essence

2 eggs

3 ripe bananas, roughly chopped

105 g (3/4 cup) roasted hazelnuts, roughly chopped

sifted icing (confectioners') sugar, for dusting

1 Preheat the oven to 160°C (310°F/Gas 2). Lightly grease a deep 23 cm (9 inch) round springform tin and line the base with baking paper. Put the apricots into a small bowl. Pour the orange juice over them and allow to soak for 30 minutes.

2 Sift the flour, bicarbonate of soda and spices into a large bowl. Put the sugar, olive oil and vanilla into a small bowl and beat with an electric beater until thick and creamy. Add the eggs one at a time, beating well after each addition. Pour the mixture into the dry ingredients and gently fold in using a large metal spoon.

3 Add the apricots along with the juice, bananas and nuts. Stir gently to combine. Spoon the mixture into the cake tin and bake for 1 1/2 hours or until firm and golden brown on top. Allow the cake to stand for 30 minutes before turning out onto a wire rack to cool. Dust with icing sugar before serving.

Gingerbread cake

Preparation time:

15 mins

Cooking time:

1 hour 10 mins

MAKES A LARGE RECTANGULAR CAKE

185 g (1 1/2 cups) plain (all-purpose) flour

60 g (1/2 cup) self-raising flour

1 teaspoon bicarbonate of soda

1 tablespoon ground ginger

1 teaspoon mixed spice

230 g (1 cup) soft brown sugar

125 ml (1/2 cup) olive oil

350 g (1 cup) golden syrup

2 eggs, lightly beaten

250 ml (1 cup) milk

Lemon icing

250 g (2 cups) icing (confectioners') sugar

juice of 1–2 lemons

75 g (2 1/2 oz) shelled pistachio nuts, roughly chopped

1   Preheat the oven to 180°C (350°F/Gas 4). Lightly grease a deep 28 x 22 cm (11 x 9 inch) tin and line the base with baking paper.

2   Sift the flours, bicarbonate of soda, ginger and mixed spice into a large bowl. Add the sugar and mix to combine. Make a well in the centre, then pour in the oil, syrup, eggs and milk. Beat with a wooden spoon until just combined.

3   Pour the mixture into the prepared tin and smooth the surface. Bake for 1 hour 10 minutes or until a skewer comes out clean when inserted into the centre of the cake. Cool the cake on a wire rack for 10 minutes before turning out.

4   To make the lemon icing, sift the icing sugar into a medium-sized bowl. Gradually add the lemon juice and stir continuously until a thin, runny icing forms. Pour over the gingerbread then sprinkle with chopped nuts.

Winter

Winter
warmers

Make the most of the cooler weather and warm up with

braises, stews and casseroles and other hearty fare.

What should I cook my casserole in?

As a general rule, the heavier the dish, the better, as these dishes and pots will
warm up slowly and distribute the heat more evenly. However,
if using something that's on the thin side, turn the heat
down a little when simmering and stir occasionally to make
sure the food is not sticking to the bottom of the dish.

Braises, stews and casseroles

Wet cookery is the general name given to food
cooked covered in a liquid, but the differences
between styles are minimal. A braise is when liquid
is added to meat after it has been browned in a little
butter and/or oil, and it can be cooked on the top of
the stove or in the oven. A stew is a pot on top of the
stove and a casserole is a covered dish in the oven.
All methods produce tender food in an aromatic sauce.

Staying healthy in winter

In winter it's vital to protect against the illnesses that often accompany the season and put a lot of stress on your immune system.

To feel good, it's essential to eat foods packed with nutrients that will boost your immune system. These include plenty of fresh fruit and vegetables, plus three to four serves of lean red meat a week.

Red meat is a valuable source of zinc, which is vital for a healthy immune system. As well as protecting against colds and flu, zinc helps keep hair and skin in good condition and has been proven to aid the body's natural healing processes.

Lean red meat is ideal for growing bodies. Along with zinc, it's packed with vitamin B12 for brain performance and concentration, iron for alertness and energy, and protein for growth and development. Enough to get any active child through the winter months!

Nothing takes the chill off a freezing winter's evening like a steaming bowl of stew that's hearty and wholesome.

Curried parsnip soup

Preparation time:

20 mins

Cooking time:

50 mins

SERVES 4

1 tablespoon oil

25 g (1 oz) butter

1 onion, finely chopped

8 cm (3 inch) piece fresh ginger, finely chopped

2 cloves garlic, finely chopped

60 g (1/4 cup) mild curry paste

2 Granny Smith apples, peeled, cored and quartered

1 kg (2 lb 4 oz) parsnips, peeled and roughly chopped

2 litres (8 cups) vegetable or chicken stock

300 ml (10 1/2 fl oz) cream

salt and freshly ground black pepper

sprigs rosemary, to garnish

1 Heat the oil and butter in a large heavy-based pan. Add the onion, ginger, garlic and curry paste. Stir until well combined. Cook over a medium heat for 2–3 minutes, or until the onion is soft. Add the apple and parsnip and stir together well.

2 Cook the apple and parsnip mixture for 2–3 minutes or until the vegetables start to brown. Pour the stock into the pan, stir to combine and bring slowly to the boil. Reduce the heat and simmer, covered, for 35–40 minutes or until the parsnips are tender.

3 Remove from the heat and allow to cool slightly. Process the soup in a food processor until smooth. Return the soup to the pan and bring slowly to the boil. Reduce to a simmer, then add the cream, salt and pepper. Stir until well combined. Cook for 1–2 minutes longer. Serve topped with rosemary leaves and Rosemary and garlic toast (page 287).

Rosemary and garlic toast

Parsnip chips

Rosemary and garlic toast

Preparation time:

10 mins

Cooking time:

15 mins

SERVES 4

1 baguette

125 ml (½ cup) olive oil

2 cloves garlic, finely chopped

½ bunch rosemary, sprigs only

Preheat the oven to 180°C (350°F/Gas 4). Line a baking tray with baking paper. Thinly slice the bread and lay out on the prepared tray. Pour the oil into a small bowl, then stir in the garlic. Brush the oil mixture over the slices of bread. Sprinkle with rosemary sprigs. Bake for 15–20 minutes or until golden brown and crisp. Remove and allow to cool.

Parsnip chips

Preparation time:

20 mins

Cooking time:

10 mins

SERVES 4

500 g (1 lb 2 oz) parsnips

vegetable oil, for deep-frying

salt

Peel and trim the parsnips. Using a sharp knife, slice the parsnips into wafer-thin rounds. Place in a bowl of cold water and leave to stand for 10 minutes. Pour the oil into a pan to one-third full. Heat the oil. Drain the parsnip rounds and dry in a clean tea towel or paper towel. Drop 3–4 rounds at a time into the hot oil. When golden brown, remove the rounds from the oil with a slotted spoon. Drain well on crumpled greaseproof paper. Sprinkle with salt and serve.

Step by Step
Chilli beef

Preparation time:

35 mins

Cooking time:

2 hours

COOK'S TIP

Part of the fun of chilli beef
is the little extras served on
the side. We've served it
with coriander, sour cream,
enchiladas, chopped avocado
and lime wedges. You could
also add some chilli flakes if
you like things really hot.

SERVES 6

2 tablespoons olive oil

1 birdseye chilli, chopped

2 red banana chillies, chopped

2 tablespoons sweet paprika

1 tablespoon ground cumin

1 tablespoon ground coriander

2 cloves garlic, chopped

1 kg (2 lb 4 oz) skirt steak, trimmed
    and cut into 8 cm (3 inch) cubes

2 x 425 g (15 oz) cans chopped tomatoes

375 ml (1½ cups) beef stock

125 g (½ cup) tomato paste (purée)

2 tablespoons soft brown sugar

2 tablespoons brown vinegar

2 large red capsicums (peppers), chopped

2 x 425 g (15 oz) cans kidney beans, drained
    and thoroughly rinsed (for at least 2 minutes)

Step 1

Heat the oil in a large
heavy-based pan, then
add the chillies, paprika,
cumin, coriander and
garlic and stir over a low
heat for 1 minute. Add the
meat in batches, turning
to coat on each side.

Step 2

Add the tomatoes, stock,
tomato paste, sugar and
vinegar and stir. Reduce
the heat to medium–low
and simmer for 1½ hours,
stirring occasionally,
without allowing to boil.

Step 3

Remove the meat from
the pan and put on a
large plate. Use two
long-pronged forks to tear
each piece of meat into
long, thin shreds. Return
the meat to the pan as
you go. Stir well.

Step 4

Add the capsicum and
beans to the pan and stir
well. Cook, uncovered,
for 5 minutes. To serve,
spoon the beef into a
bowl and top with
coriander, sour cream
and chilli flakes, if desired.

Tarragon chicken with potatoes and asparagus

Preparation time:

25 minutes

Cooking time:

1½ hours

COOK'S TIP

Garlic becomes quite sweet and mellow when it is cooked whole in the oven. After cooking, squeeze the garlic from each clove and spread over the chicken for a sweet flavour.

SERVES 4

2 slices white crusty bread, cut in half

1 lemon, cut into quarters

10 g (½ bunch) thyme

1.6 kg (3 lb 8 oz) chicken, giblets, neck and pieces
    of fat removed, washed with salt water, patted dry

60 g (2¼ oz) butter, softened

½ bunch tarragon

salt and freshly ground black pepper

1 whole bulb garlic, cut in half (see Cook's tip)

250 ml (1 cup) chicken stock

1 kg (2 lb 4 oz) sebago potatoes, peeled

30 g (1 oz) butter, melted

1 tablespoon olive oil

310 g (2 bunches) asparagus, trimmed

extra 20 g (½ oz) butter

100 g (3½ oz) roasted hazelnuts, roughly chopped

1 Preheat the oven to 180°C (350°F/Gas 4). Put the bread, lemon and thyme in the cavity of the chicken. Put the butter in a small bowl, add the tarragon, salt and pepper and mix. Gently loosen the skin from the breast. Push the butter mixture evenly under the skin on both sides of the breast. Bring the skin back over the breast section. Tie the legs together with a piece of string.

2 Put the chicken in a deep, heavy ovenproof dish. Put half a bulb of garlic on each side and pour on the chicken stock. Cover with a lid or a sheet of aluminium foil. Cook, covered, for 1 hour. Remove the cover from the chicken and cook for another 30–35 minutes or until the juices run clear. Stand for 10 minutes before carving. Serve the chicken with potatoes and asparagus.

3 To prepare the potatoes, use a large sharp knife to make 1 cm (½ inch) deep cuts at 2 mm (⅛ inch) intervals, without cutting all the way through. Place in a bowl of salted water and stand for 20 minutes. Drain the potatoes well. Place in a baking dish and brush with a combination of melted butter and olive oil. Bake for 50–60 minutes or until the potatoes are golden brown and cooked through.

4 Boil the asparagus in a small amount of water until just tender. Meanwhile, heat the extra butter in a small pan, add the hazelnuts and cook until dark golden. Pour the butter and hazelnuts over the drained asparagus just before serving.

Chicken and mushrooms with thyme cream sauce

Preparation time:

15 mins

Cooking time:

20 mins

COOK'S TIP

Delicate and tender, enoki mushrooms have tiny button caps and long thread-like stems. They grow in clusters with a solid base and are sold in their clumps. Just trim away the base before using them.

SERVES 4

4 single chicken breast fillets

60 g (1/2 cup) plain (all-purpose) flour

salt and freshly ground black pepper

30 g (1 oz) butter

2 tablespoons olive oil

extra 30 g (1 oz) butter

200 g (7 oz) Swiss brown mushrooms, sliced

200 g (7 oz) button mushrooms, sliced

2 cloves garlic, finely chopped

100 g (3½ oz) enoki mushrooms, trimmed (see Cook's tip)

125 ml (1/2 cup) white wine

300 ml (10½ fl oz) cream

10 g (1/2 bunch) fresh thyme, sprigs only

extra sprigs thyme, for garnish

1 Lay your hand flat over each fillet and, using a sharp knife, slice through lengthways to form two thin fillets. Sprinkle the flour onto a sheet of baking paper and season. Coat the fillets in flour, then dust off any excess.

2 Add the butter and oil to a large heavy-based pan and heat until the butter starts to foam. Add the fillets, a couple at a time, and cook on a medium heat for 2–3 minutes on each side or until the chicken is cooked through. Lift the chicken onto a plate, cover with foil and set aside. Keep warm. Remove any excess oil from the pan and wipe it clean with paper towel.

3 Melt the extra butter in the pan. Add the Swiss brown mushrooms, button mushrooms and garlic. Cook for 1–2 minutes or until the mushrooms start to soften. Add the enoki mushrooms and cook briefly until just wilted.

4 Pour the white wine into the pan and cook, stirring, for 1–2 minutes. Add the cream, thyme, and salt and pepper. Bring the sauce to a simmer and cook for 2–3 minutes longer.

5 Return the cooked chicken to the pan and turn to coat with the cream sauce. Place the chicken on serving plates and spoon some of the mushrooms and sauce over each plate. Garnish each serving with extra thyme sprigs.

Lamb and spinach curry

Preparation time:

20 mins

Cooking time:

1 hour 20 mins

COOK'S TIP

This curry is full of flavour
and the meat will melt in your
mouth. Serve it with naan bread
or spoon it over steamed
basmati rice.

SERVES 4

2 teaspoons cumin seeds

2 teaspoons coriander seeds

8 cardamom pods, bruised

8 black peppercorns

1/2 teaspoon chilli flakes

1 tablespoon ground turmeric

1 tablespoon garam masala

3 cloves garlic, finely chopped

8 cm (3 inch) piece ginger, finely chopped

1 onion, finely chopped

1 tablespoon oil

1 kg (2 lb 4 oz) lamb, cubed

500 g (1 lb 2 oz) thick plain yoghurt

100 g (3 handfuls) baby spinach leaves, washed

salt

a little extra oil

mango chutney, for serving

fresh mint leaves, for serving

1 Dry-fry the cumin, coriander seeds, cardamom, peppercorns and chilli flakes in a frypan over a low heat for 1 minute or until aromatic. Spoon into a small food processor, then add the turmeric, garam masala, garlic, ginger and onion. Process until well combined.

2 Heat the oil in a large, heavy-based pan. Add the spice mixture to the pan and cook for 1 minute. Add the lamb to the pan, stir to coat in the spice mixture and then cook for 2–3 minutes.

3 Add the yoghurt to the pan a spoonful at a time, stirring well between each addition. Simmer for 1 1/4 hours or until the meat is tender (The time will vary slightly depending on the size of the lamb cubes and the pan's dimensions). The meat should be tender and the sauce thick and creamy.

4 Add the spinach leaves to the meat, stir well and cook until the spinach is just wilted. Season to taste with salt. Top the lamb with some mango chutney and mint.

Beef and red wine casserole

Preparation time:

25 mins

Cooking time:

2 hours

SERVES 4

2 tablespoons oil

25 g (1 oz) butter

1 kg (2 lb 4 oz) beef, cut into 3 cm (1¼ inch) cubes

8 bulb spring onions, trimmed

3 slices bacon, rind removed and roughly chopped

extra 60 g (2¼ oz) butter

30 g (¼ cup) plain (all-purpose) flour

375 ml (1½ cups) red wine

375 ml (1½ cups) beef stock

2 bay leaves

salt and freshly ground black pepper

1 Preheat the oven to 180°C (350°F/Gas 4). Heat the oil and butter in a large pan or heavy-based casserole dish. Add half the beef in small batches over medium to high heat until browned on all sides. Remove the beef from the pan. Repeat with the rest of the meat.

2 Add the spring onions to the pan and cook until they turn light brown. Add the bacon and cook until crisp. Remove from the pan. Melt the extra butter in the pan. Add the flour, stirring continuously until golden brown. Remove the pan from the heat and slowly pour in the wine and stock, stirring continuously until well combined. Return the pan to the heat, add the bay leaves, salt and pepper and stir continuously until the sauce comes to the boil and thickens. Return the meat and bacon to the pan.

3 Cook, covered, in the oven for 1 hour. Add the spring onions. Cover and cook for a further 30 minutes or until the meat is tender. Serve.

Lamb shanks in orange sauce

Preparation time:

15 mins

Cooking time:

2½ hours

SERVES 6

1 tablespoon oil

6 frenched lamb shanks

1 large onion, finely chopped

2 cloves garlic, finely chopped

strips of zest from 1 orange (pith removed)

250 ml (1 cup) orange juice (juice of 3–4 oranges)

375 ml (1½ cups) beef stock

425 g (15 oz) can chopped tomatoes

2 bay leaves

1 teaspoon dried thyme

salt and freshly ground black pepper

mashed potato, for serving

sprigs thyme, to garnish

1   Heat the oil in a large pan or large heatproof casserole over a medium to high heat. Add half the shanks and brown on all sides. Remove from the pan. Brown the remaining shanks and remove them also.

2   Reduce the heat to medium, add the onion and garlic and cook for about 2 minutes. Add the orange zest, orange juice, stock, tomatoes, bay leaves, thyme, salt and pepper. Stir to combine. Bring slowly to the boil. Reduce to a simmer and return the shanks to the pan. Cover and cook for 2–2½ hours or until the meat is tender. Alternatively, cover and place the casserole in a 180°C (350°F/Gas 4) oven and cook for 2–2½ hours.

3   For a thicker sauce, remove the shanks from the pan, bring the sauce slowly to the boil, reduce to a simmer and cook until reduced by about one-third. Serve the shanks with mashed potato, then spoon over the sauce and top with fresh thyme.

Chicken with lemon and olives

Preparation time:

25 mins

Cooking time:

55 mins

COOK'S TIP

To make couscous, bring 1 litre (4 cups) chicken stock slowly to the boil in a pan. Remove from the heat. Stir in 500 g (1 lb 2 oz) couscous. Cover and stand for 5 minutes. Stir in some chopped parsley and 25 g (1 oz) butter.

SERVES 6

1 teaspoon saffron threads

125 ml (½ cup) olive oil

2 kg (4 lb 8 oz) assorted chicken pieces (with the bone in and skin on), cut into serving-size pieces

1 large onion, finely chopped

3 cloves garlic, finely chopped

1 tablespoon sweet paprika

2 teaspoons ground cumin

2 teaspoons ground coriander

500 ml (2 cups) chicken stock

strip of lemon peel

juice of 1 lemon

extra lemon, thinly sliced

175 g (1 cup) green olives

1   Put the saffron threads in a small dry pan and cook, stirring, for 1 minute. Remove and place in a small bowl. Press with the end of a wooden spoon until the saffron crumbles.

2   Heat the oil in a large pan, add the chicken, skin side down, in a single layer and cook until golden brown. Turn and cook for a further 3–4 minutes. Remove from the pan and set aside. Add the onion, garlic, paprika, cumin and coriander. Stir well and cook over a low heat for 1 minute.

3   Add the stock, strip of lemon peel, lemon juice and saffron to the onion mixture and stir to combine. Cook for 1–2 minutes, add the chicken and simmer, covered, for 40 minutes or until the chicken is tender. Add the lemon and olives and cook for a further 5 minutes. Serve the chicken with couscous, if desired (see Cook's tip).

Step by Step
Meat pie

Preparation time:

25 mins

Cooking time:

1¼ hours

COOK'S TIP

The pie funnel (or blackbird, as it's known) is there to let the steam out of the filling as it cooks and prevent the pastry from going soft. If you don't have a blackbird, make a couple of small deep cuts on top of the pastry after it has been glazed.

SERVES 6

40 g (⅓ cup) plain (all-purpose) flour, seasoned

2 teaspoons dried mixed herbs

1 kg (2 lb 4 oz) trimmed and cubed chuck steak

500 g (1 lb 2 oz) potatoes, peeled and cubed

2 bay leaves

2 tablespoons olive oil

1 large onion, roughly chopped

60 ml (¼ cup) Worcestershire sauce

125 g (½ cup) tomato sauce

400 g (14 oz) can beef consommé

extra 125 g (1 cup) plain (all-purpose) flour, sifted

125 g (1 cup) self-raising flour, sifted

125 g (4½ oz) butter, chopped and chilled

125 ml (½ cup) chilled water

30 g (½ cup) sprigs parsley

1 egg, lightly beaten, for glazing

Step 1
Preheat the oven to 180°C (350°F/Gas 4). Put the flour, dried herbs and beef in a large plastic bag. Toss. Transfer to a 2.5 litre (10 cup), 8 cm (3 inches) deep ovenproof dish.

Step 2
Mix in the potato, then add the bay leaves. Heat the oil in a pan, add the onion and cook over a medium heat until soft. Add the sauces and consommé and stir. Bring to the boil, reduce to a simmer and cook for 8–10 minutes. Cool. Pour into the ovenproof dish.

Step 3
Put the flours and butter in a food processor and mix until the mixture resembles fine breadcrumbs. Add the water and parsley and process until a rough ball forms. Knead the pastry into a ball on a lightly floured surface.

Step 4
Roll out the pastry on a floured surface to fit the dish, and cut a cross in the centre. Sit the blackbird in the middle of the filling. Lay the pastry on top, allowing the blackbird to poke through. Brush with egg. Bake for 1¼ hours. Stand for 5 minutes, then serve.

Lamb with cardamom crust and sesame pumpkin

Preparation time:

10 mins

Cooking time:

30 mins

COOK'S TIPS

Cardamom is a versatile spice that teams well with both sweet and savoury foods. It has an unmistakable pungent flavour and can have a slight lemony or eucalyptus tang that is very refreshing to the palate. The seeds should look fresh and have a strong aroma.

SERVES 4

4 slices white bread, roughly torn into pieces

2 teaspoons cardamom seeds (see Cook's tip)

60 g (½ cup) finely chopped walnuts

30 g (½ bunch) chives, finely chopped

40 g (½ bunch) mint, finely chopped

grated zest and juice of 1 orange

1 tablespoon olive oil

salt and freshly ground black pepper

4 x 4 lamb cutlet racks, well trimmed

sprigs of mint, to garnish

Sesame pumpkin

1 kg (2 lb 4 oz) pumpkin, peeled and
    cut into 3 cm (1¼ inch) pieces

2 teaspoons sesame oil

80 g (⅓ cup) soft brown sugar

2 teaspoons sesame seeds

1 Preheat the oven to 200°C (400°F/Gas 6). Place the bread in a food processor with the cardamom seeds and process until coarse crumbs are formed. Scoop into a medium-sized bowl.

2 Add the walnuts, chives, mint, zest, juice and oil. Season with salt and pepper, and mix to combine. Press equal amounts of the bread mixture onto the back of each lamb rack. Put the racks in a baking dish. Bake for 25–30 minutes. Serve the lamb with Sesame pumpkin on the side and garnish with a few sprigs of fresh mint.

3 To make the Sesame pumpkin, put the chopped pumpkin pieces in an ovenproof dish. Sprinkle with the sesame oil and brown sugar and top with sesame seeds. Bake for 25–30 minutes or until the pumpkin is tender.

Golden syrup and ginger dumplings

Preparation time:

15 mins

Cooking time:

30 mins

SERVES 6

500 ml (2 cups) water

165 g (3/4 cup) white sugar

80 g (1/3 cup) golden syrup

60 g (2 1/4 oz) butter

80 g (1/4 cup) ginger and lime marmalade

125 g (1 cup) self-raising flour

2 teaspoons ground ginger

extra 60 g (2 1/4 oz) butter, chopped

100 ml (3 1/2 fl oz) milk

extra flour, for shaping

125 g (4 1/2 oz) good-quality dark chocolate,
   broken into cubes

ice cream or cream, for serving

1   Place the water, sugar, golden syrup, butter and marmalade in a medium-sized, heavy-based pan. Stir over a medium heat until the butter, sugar and marmalade dissolve. Bring slowly to the boil, then reduce to a fast simmer.

2   Sift the flour and ground ginger into a bowl, then add the chopped butter. Rub the butter into the flour until the mixture resembles fine breadcrumbs. Make a well in the centre, pour in the milk and stir with a table knife until the mixture forms a dough.

3   Dust a little flour on a workbench. Place the dough on the surface and shape into a log about 18 cm (7 inches) long. Divide the log into 12 even pieces. Sit a piece of chocolate on each piece, then roll each piece into a ball, making sure the chocolate is in the centre and covered by the dough.

4   Put the balls into the simmering golden syrup mixture. Cover and cook for 20 minutes. Serve the dumplings and syrup with scoops of ice cream or a spoonful of cream.

Self-saucing butterscotch pudding

Preparation time:	SERVES 6
15 mins	155 g (1¼ cups) self-raising flour, sifted
	115 g (½ cup) firmly packed soft brown sugar
Cooking time:	100 g (3½ oz) butter, melted
50 mins	125 ml (½ cup) milk
	1 egg
	1 teaspoon vanilla essence
	extra 185 g (1 cup) loosely packed soft brown sugar
	40 g (⅓ cup) malted milk drink powder
	1 tablespoon cornflour (cornstarch)
	375 ml (1½ cups) boiling water
	125 ml (½ cup) cream

Step 1
Preheat the oven to 180°C (350°F/Gas 4). Brush a 1.25 litre (5 cup) ovenproof dish with melted butter. Put the flour and brown sugar in a mixing bowl and mix with a wooden spoon to combine. Pour the melted butter, milk, egg and vanilla essence into a jug and beat with a fork until combined.

Step 2
Make a well in the centre of the dry ingredients. Pour in the combined milk mixture and beat with a wooden spoon until the mixture is smooth and well combined. Spoon the mixture into the prepared dish and smooth over the surface.

Step 3
Put the extra brown sugar, malted milk drink powder and cornflour in a small bowl and mix with a fork until well combined. Sprinkle this mixture evenly over the top of the pudding mixture.

Step 4
Pour the boiling water into a jug, add the cream and stir to combine. Carefully pour the cream mixture over the back of a large metal spoon onto the brown sugar mixture. Bake for 45–50 minutes. Serve hot or warm with a scoop of honeycomb ice cream.

Baked pasta

There is nothing more satisfying than a plate of pasta – especially when it's baked. It must be those crunchy bits that make it such a treat. But the best thing about baked pasta is that it goes a long way. It makes a filling meal for the whole family and is a great stand-by when friends drop in. Simply make it the day before, store it in the fridge and reheat it in the oven.

Fresh sage

Sage has the most wonderful soft, silver, velvety leaves. It has a very distinctive, strong aromatic flavour that's perfect with the ingredients which traditionally go with pasta, like tomato, cheese and smoked meats. Choose sprigs with soft, unblemished leaves. Most greengrocers sell sage either by the bunch or in small containers.

Pasta for baking

Choose pasta that has 'strong walls' – a phrase used to describe very thick pasta. It should still be *al dente* – or firm to the bite – after baking, so only just cook it on the stove, as it will be heated through a second time in the oven.

Lasagne is the pasta most commonly used for baking but you can also try short pasta like penne and tortiglioni, and long tubular shapes like bucatini.

Here's the good oil

Have you ever been told to add a little oil to the water when you cook pasta? Well, it's not such a good idea after all because the oil prevents the sauce from sticking to the pasta. The best way to stop pasta from sticking together is to cook it in a big pot of boiling, salted water.

Bring these baked pasta dishes to the table hot, bubbling and smelling absolutely irresistible.

Pastitsio

Preparation time:

45 mins

Cooking time:

1 hour 45 mins

SERVES 10

1 tablespoon olive oil

500 g (1 lb 2 oz) minced (ground) veal

3 cloves garlic, finely chopped

1 large onion, finely chopped

2 x 450 g (1 lb) cans chopped tomatoes

375 ml (1½ cups) white wine

125 g (½ cup) tomato paste (purée)

1 cinnamon stick

3 bay leaves

180 g (6 oz) butter, chopped

125 g (1 cup) plain (all-purpose) flour

1.5 litres (6 cups) milk

½ teaspoon ground nutmeg

salt and freshly ground black pepper

3 eggs, lightly beaten

185 g (1½ cups) grated Cheddar cheese

500 g (1 lb 2 oz) maccheroni (macaroni) or small tubular pasta

1 To make the meat sauce, heat the oil in a large, heavy-based saucepan. Add the meat and cook, stirring, for 4–5 minutes or until it starts to change colour. Add the garlic and onion and cook for 2–3 minutes or until the onion starts to soften. Add the tomatoes, wine and tomato paste, then stir well. Add the cinnamon and bay leaves. Cook for 40–45 minutes until a thick sauce has formed.

2 Preheat the oven to 180°C (350°F/Gas 4). To make the cheese sauce, melt the butter in a large, heavy-based pan. Remove from the heat, add the flour and stir. Return to the stove and cook over a low heat for 1–2 minutes. Remove from the heat and gradually stir in the milk until the mixture is smooth. Return to the heat and whisk continually until the mixture comes to the boil. Stir in the nutmeg, then season. Simmer for 5 minutes or until the sauce is thick and glossy. Remove from the heat and stand for 5 minutes before adding the eggs and cheese. Beat well.

3 Cook the pasta in a large pot of boiling, salted water until just tender. Drain well. Return to the pot, add the veal sauce and toss to combine.

4 Grease a large ovenproof dish, about 38 x 26 x 6 cm (16 x 10½ x 2½ inches). Place the combined pasta and veal sauce mixture in the prepared dish. Pour the cheese sauce over the top and spread evenly. Bake for 55–60 minutes. Allow to stand for 10 minutes before serving. Cut into squares and serve.

Tomato and cheese pasta

Preparation time:

10 mins

Cooking time:

35 mins

SERVES 4

500 g (1 lb 2 oz) bucatini or penne pasta

100 g (3½ oz) gorgonzola cheese, crumbled

100 g (3½ oz) Gruyère cheese, grated

100 g (3½ oz) mozzarella cheese, grated

250 g (1 punnet) small cherry tomatoes

1 Preheat the oven to 180°C (350°F/Gas 4). Cook the pasta in boiling, salted water until just tender. Drain, leaving a little cooking water clinging to the pasta.

2 Return the pasta to the pan and add the gorgonzola, Gruyère, mozzarella and tomatoes. Stir until well combined. Spoon into a large, ovenproof dish. Bake for 30–35 minutes or until golden brown and crispy on top. Allow to stand for 5 minutes. Serve immediately.

Pumpkin lasagne

Preparation time:

30 mins

Cooking time:

1 hour 20 mins

SERVES 6

1 kg (2 lb 4 oz) pumpkin, peeled and chopped

2 tablespoons olive oil

salt and freshly ground black pepper

1 tablespoon oil

1 large onion, finely chopped

15 g (1/2 bunch) chives, finely chopped

15 g (1/2 bunch) sage, finely chopped

1/2 teaspoon ground nutmeg

350 g (12 oz) fresh ricotta cheese

150 g (1 cup) grated mozzarella cheese

12 dried lasagne sheets

300 ml (101/2 fl oz) light thickened cream

50 g (1/2 cup) grated Parmesan cheese

100 g (31/2 oz) butter

extra 15 g (1/2 bunch) fresh sage leaves

1 Preheat the oven to 180°C (350°F/Gas 4). Line an ovenproof tray with baking paper. Grease a deep, rectangular ovenproof dish. Put the pumpkin in a bowl, add the oil and toss to combine. Transfer to the prepared tray. Season. Bake the pumpkin for 20–25 minutes. Remove from the oven and allow to cool. Transfer to a food processor and process until smooth. Spoon the puréed pumpkin into a large bowl.

2 Heat the oil in a small pan. Add the onion and cook until softened. Remove from the heat. Add the onion, chives, sage and nutmeg to the pumpkin. Stir to combine.

3 Put three lasagne sheets in the base of the prepared dish, then top with one-third of the pumpkin mixture, one-third of the ricotta and one-third of the mozzarella. Repeat this process twice, finishing with three sheets of lasagne. Pour the cream over the lasagne and top with Parmesan. Bake for 35 minutes or until golden and bubbly on top. Stand for 10 minutes before serving.

4 Melt the butter in a small pan. Add the sage leaves and fry gently until the leaves are crisp and the butter is golden brown. Pour over the lasagne and then serve.

Italian sausage and fennel pasta

Preparation time:

25 mins

Cooking time:

35 mins

COOK'S TIP

Italian sausages are available from most delicatessens. Some are hot and spicy, and some are flavoured with fennel or fresh herbs. Any of these flavours could be used for this dish.

SERVES 4

500 g (1 lb 2 oz) tortiglioni or penne rigate

6 Italian sausages

3 baby fennel, thinly sliced

60 g (2¼ oz) butter

30 g (¼ cup) plain (all-purpose) flour

250 ml (1 cup) chicken stock

250 ml (1 cup) white wine

125 ml (½ cup) grated Parmesan cheese

freshly ground black pepper

1 Cook the pasta in boiling, salted water until just tender. Drain, leaving a little water clinging to the pasta. Preheat the oven to 180°C (350°F/Gas 4) and lightly grease a large, ovenproof dish.

2 Place the sausages in a heavy-based pan and cook for 3–4 minutes or until almost cooked through and browned. Remove from the pan and drain on paper towel. Add the fennel to the pan and cook until just tender. Remove.

3 Melt the butter in the pan, then remove from the heat, add the flour and stir until well combined. Slowly add the stock and wine to the mixture, stirring or whisking until smooth. Return to the heat and cook, stirring, until the sauce boils and thickens. Simmer for 1–2 minutes, then remove from the heat.

4 Using tongs, hold each sausage firmly on a wooden board. With a sharp knife, cut the skin down the length of the sausage and scrape out the meat. Discard the lining. Add the sausage meat, fennel and sauce to the pasta, then toss to combine. Spoon the mixture into the prepared dish. Sprinkle with Parmesan cheese. Bake for 30–35 minutes or until heated through and golden. Season with black pepper.

rice

Rice has been a staple around the world for a long time and remains one of the most popular foods in many cuisines. Keep a packet of rice in the pantry and you will have the base for many meals, drawing on cuisines from all over the world.

Cooking rice by the absorption method

To steam rice for four, put 200 g (7 oz) of rice in a colander or sieve and wash under cold running water until the water runs clear. Put rice in a heavy-based saucepan with a tight-fitting lid. When preparing to boil rice, ensure the water level is 2 cm (3/4 inch) above the rice. To do this, rest your thumb on top of the rice and fill the pot with enough water to reach just above the first joint of your thumb.

Cook rice on a high heat until the water has evaporated and small tunnels form in the rice. If you have an electric stove top, turn off the heat (an electric hotplate still has enough heat to cook the rice when turned off). If you have a gas stove top, reduce the burner to a very low heat and cook, covered, for 10–12 minutes or until the rice is tender. Remove from the heat and stir with a fork before serving. Both long- and short- to medium-grain rice can be cooked in this way.

Types of rice

Many different types of rice are now readily available in the supermarket. Basically, rice can be divided into two categories: long-grain and short- to medium-grain. There are also different types of rice within these categories.

The long-grain category includes the aromatic rice jasmine, which is served with Thai food, and basmati, which is perfect with Indian. Plain white long-grain is extensively used in Asian and other cookery.

Short- and medium-grain rice is plump and moist when cooked, with a certain degree of stickiness. The Japanese use short-grain rice in sushi and it's also the most commonly eaten rice across China, where its stickiness makes it easy to eat with chopsticks. Short-grain rice is used in the making of paella, the popular Spanish dish, and is the best for a good old-fashioned rice pudding.

Arborio is the medium-grain rice used in the Italian speciality, risotto. It has an almost pearl-like appearance and a creamy texture when cooked.

You can buy brown rice in both long- and short-grain forms which can be substituted for any rice. Brown rice has a nutty flavour and a coarse, chewy texture. Remember, it will take much longer to cook.

Rice is eaten daily by over 300 billion people around the world.

Sweet potato pilaf

Preparation time:

20 mins

Cooking time:

25 mins

SERVES 4

1 tablespoon olive oil

1 onion, chopped

300 g (1 1/2 cups) basmati rice

1 cinnamon stick, split

6 cardamom pods, split

500 g (1 lb 2 oz) sweet potato, cut into
   2.5 cm (1 inch) pieces

625 ml (2 1/2 cups) chicken or vegetable stock

60 g (1/2 cup) raisins

65 g (1/2 cup) shelled pistachios, roughly chopped

1 Heat the oil in a heavy-based pan. Add the onion and rice and cook, stirring, over a medium heat until the rice is coated in oil. Add the cinnamon stick, cardamom and sweet potato and stir to combine.

2 Add the stock and raisins and stir well. Cover and cook over a low heat for 20 minutes or until the sweet potato is tender and the liquid has evaporated. Serve the pilaf topped with pistachios.

Salmon kedgeree

Preparation time:

15 mins

Cooking time:

10 mins

SERVES 4

200 g (1 cup) basmati rice

500 g (1 lb 2 oz) salmon fillets

1 small lemon, sliced

60 g (2¼ oz) butter

1 onion, finely chopped

2 tablespoons mild curry powder

juice of 1 small lemon

2 hard-boiled eggs, roughly chopped

salt and freshly ground black pepper

parsley sprigs, to garnish

2 extra hard-boiled eggs, cut into quarters, for serving

buttered toast, for serving

1 Put the rice in a heavy-based pan. Rest your thumb on the rice, then add enough water to come up to the first joint of your thumb. Bring the rice to the boil and boil until all the water has evaporated and small tunnels have formed in the rice. Cover with a tight-fitting lid and cook on a very low heat for 8–10 minutes.

2 Place the salmon in a medium-sized pan. Add the lemon slices and cover with cold water. Bring to the boil, then reduce the heat and simmer for 5–6 minutes. Remove the salmon with tongs, then put on a plate. Allow to cool slightly, then flake into large pieces with a fork, removing any small bones. Cover the fish with aluminium foil to keep warm.

3 Melt the butter in a large pan. Add the onion and cook for 2–3 minutes or until soft. Add the curry powder and lemon juice, then stir until well combined. Add the cooked rice, stir with a fork until well combined and the rice is coated in curry mixture.

4 Add the salmon, egg, salt and pepper to the rice mixture. Lightly stir through until combined and heated through. Garnish with parsley sprigs. Serve with egg quarters and buttered toast.

Pea and pancetta risotto

Preparation time:	**SERVES 4**
10 mins	1 litre (4 cups) chicken or vegetable stock
	75 g (2½ oz) pancetta, roughly chopped
Cooking time:	60 g (2¼ oz) unsalted butter
20 mins	2 tablespoons olive oil
	1 onion, chopped
	extra 75 g (2½ oz) pancetta, chopped
	250 g (9 oz) arborio rice
	155 g (1 cup) frozen or fresh peas
	flaked pecorino or Parmesan cheese, to serve

1 Pour the stock into a pan and place over a low heat. The stock must be kept hot (but do not allow it to boil) while making the risotto. Put the pancetta in a small pan and cook over a low heat until crispy. Remove and set aside.

2 Put the butter and oil in a large, deep heavy-based pan. Heat until the butter starts to foam, then add the onion and extra pancetta. Stir with a wooden spoon and cook over a medium heat until the onion is softened but not browned. Add the rice and stir for 1–2 minutes until each grain of rice is well coated with butter.

3 Add the hot stock, one ladleful at a time. Cook, stirring, for 1–2 minutes or until the rice has absorbed most of the stock. Continue adding ladlefuls of stock in this way, stirring frequently until the rice is tender but firm with a creamy consistency. In the last 1–2 minutes of cooking, add the peas. Remove the pan from the heat. Cover and stand for a couple of minutes to allow the flavours to blend. Serve the risotto topped with crispy fried pancetta and flaked pecorino cheese.

Fried rice

Preparation time:

30 mins

Cooking time:

30 mins

SERVES 4

300 g (1½ cups) long-grain rice

5 pieces lup chong (see Cook's tip)

peanut oil

2 eggs, lightly beaten

250 g (9 oz) raw prawns (shrimp), peeled and chopped

2 cloves garlic, chopped

1 red capsicum (pepper), chopped

80 g (½ cup) peas

6 spring onions (scallions) sliced on the diagonal

90 g (1 cup) bean spouts, tails removed

2 tablespoons soy sauce

extra sliced spring onions (scallions), to garnish

Step 1
Place the rice in a sieve and rinse with cold water. Tip the rice into a deep, heavy-based pan. Run cold water to about 2 cm (¾ inch) above the rice. Boil and cook uncovered until all the water has evaporated. Cover, turn off the heat and stand for 15 minutes.

Step 2
To serve immediately, run a fork through the rice and spoon into a bowl. For fried rice, place in a colander and rinse well under running cold water. Drain well, spread on a flat tray and stand for 15 minutes. Refrigerate overnight for best results.

Step 3
Place the lup chong in a steamer and cook until tender. Remove from the steamer and slice thinly. Heat the wok and add 1 tablespoon of peanut oil. When hot, add the eggs and quickly swirl. Cook for 1 minute. Remove from the wok, roll and then slice thinly.

Step 4
Heat a little oil, add the lup chong and cook rapidly. Add the prawns and garlic and stir-fry. Add the rice, capsicum, peas, spring onions, bean sprouts and soy sauce. Return the egg and combine until heated through. Top with the extra sliced spring onions.

Rice pudding

Preparation time:

10 mins

Cooking time:

2 hours

Rosewater gives a delicate rose flavour to the rice pudding. It is available from most supermarkets and delicatessens.

SERVES 4

300 ml (10½ fl oz) cream

500 ml (2 cups) milk

100 g (½ cup) medium-grain white rice

80 g (⅓ cup) caster (superfine) sugar

2 tablespoons rosewater (see Cook's tip)

½ teaspoon ground nutmeg

1 Preheat the oven to 160°C (310°F/Gas 2). Lightly grease a deep 1 litre (4 cup) ovenproof dish. Place all the ingredients in the dish and stir gently to combine. Bake for 30 minutes.

2 Remove from the oven, stir well, then return to oven. Bake for a further 1½ hours or until the rice is tender and the liquid is absorbed and a brown skin has formed on the surface of the rice.

All about
dark chocolate

Dark chocolate is a must in every pantry.

It can be turned into the most wonderful

cakes, biscuits and desserts, and is perfect

to nibble on when nothing else will satisfy.

Choose a good-quality brand of chocolate.

Sure, it may be a bit more expensive, but

good chocolate will ensure your finished

recipes are totally delicious.

Make your own rich fudge sauce

Put 300 ml (10½ fl oz) cream, 200 g (7 oz) chopped dark chocolate and 100 g (3½ oz) roughly chopped marshmallows in a heavy-based pan. Stir over a low heat until smooth and melted. Remove from the heat and stir in 60 ml (¼ cup) Kahlúa or Tia Maria. The sauce will keep in an airtight container in the fridge for up to 3 weeks. It's perfect with Chocolate almond cake (page 335).

Handling chocolate

Chocolate is best stored in a cool dry place that's kept at a constant temperature. For example, don't store chocolate in the cupboard next to the oven. Never keep chocolate in the fridge. After you have opened a bar, always wrap it tightly in aluminium foil.

If there has been a great change in temperature, a white bloom may appear over the surface of the chocolate. This is the fat content of the chocolate rising to the surface – it won't affect the flavour or the cooking quality.

Melting chocolate

The best way to melt chocolate is to bring a small amount of water to the boil in a medium-sized pan. Remove the pan from the heat, then put the chopped chocolate in a heatproof glass bowl. Sit the bowl over the water, cover it with plastic wrap and leave to stand for about 10 minutes. Stir with a wooden spoon to ensure all the chocolate is melted and smooth. Do not allow any water, even the smallest amount, to come into contact with the melted chocolate as it will cause it to seize.

You can also melt chocolate in the microwave. Just put the chocolate pieces in a microwave-proof bowl, and cook, uncovered, on low in short bursts of 20–30 seconds. Gently stir the chocolate between bursts.

Chocolate (the darker the better) releases enzymes that are beneficial to your health.

Chocolate almond cake

Preparation time:

20 mins

Cooking time:

50 mins

SERVES 6

250 g (9 oz) dark chocolate, chopped

100 g (3½ oz) unsalted butter, chopped

125 ml (½ cup) strong black coffee

2 teaspoons vanilla essence

6 eggs, separated

115 g (½ cup) caster (superfine) sugar

200 g (7 oz) ground almonds

extra 1 tablespoon caster (superfine) sugar

sifted cocoa, for dusting

1 Preheat the oven to 180°C (350°F/Gas 4). Lightly grease a deep 20 cm (8 inch) round cake tin and line the base and sides with baking paper. Place the chocolate, butter, coffee and vanilla in a heavy-based pan and stir over a low heat until the chocolate is melted and the mixture is smooth. Remove from the heat and cool until lukewarm.

2 Put the egg yolks and sugar into a small bowl and beat with electric beaters until the mixture is light and creamy. Gradually add the chocolate mixture and beat on low until just combined. Transfer to a large bowl. Add the ground almonds and mix well. Wash and dry the beaters.

3 Place the egg whites in a large, clean, dry bowl and beat with electric beaters on high until soft peaks form. Add the extra sugar and beat for 1 minute longer.

4 Fold the egg whites into the chocolate using a large metal spoon. Pour the mixture into the prepared tin. Gently shake the tin to settle the mixture. Bake for 40–45 minutes or until cooked through when tested with a skewer inserted in the centre. Leave in the tin for 5 minutes before turning onto a wire rack to cool. Dust with sifted cocoa powder, if desired. Serve with Rich fudge sauce (page 332).

Hedgehog slice

Preparation time:

15 mins

Cooking time:

5 mins

MAKES A 20 CM (8 INCH) SQUARE SLICE

125 g (4^1/$_2$ oz) shredded wheatmeal biscuits

60 g (^{1}/$_2$ cup) walnuts, roughly chopped

80 g (^{1}/$_2$ cup) sultanas

125 g (4^1/$_2$ oz) unsalted butter

375 g (13 oz) dark chocolate, chopped

1   Lightly grease a deep 20 cm (8 inch) square tin and line with baking paper.
Break the biscuits into pieces and put in the cake tin. Add the walnuts and
sultanas and mix to combine.

2   Put the butter into a medium-sized, heavy-based pan and let it melt a little.
Add the chocolate and stir the mixture over a low heat until the chocolate
is melted and the mixture is smooth.

3   Pour the melted chocolate evenly over the biscuit base and mix to combine.
Cover with plastic wrap and refrigerate until set. Remove and stand for
30 minutes before cutting into fingers.

Chocolate chip cookies

Preparation time:

25 mins

Cooking time:

10 mins

MAKES 32 COOKIES

125 g (4¹/₂ oz) butter, chopped

250 g (9 oz) dark chocolate, chopped

3 eggs, lightly beaten

230 g (1 cup) soft brown sugar

155 g (1¹/₄ cups) plain (all-purpose) flour, sifted

60 g (¹/₂ cup) cocoa, sifted

extra 200 g (7 oz) dark chocolate, roughly chopped

60 g (¹/₂ cup) roasted hazelnuts, roughly chopped

1 Preheat the oven to 200°C (400°F/Gas 6). Line three oven trays with baking paper. Put the butter and chocolate in a small pan and stir over a low heat until the chocolate melts and the mixture is smooth. Transfer to a large bowl.

2 Add the beaten eggs and brown sugar to the chocolate mixture and stir until combined. Add the sifted flour and cocoa, extra chocolate and hazelnuts. Stir well.

3 Drop tablespoons of the mixture onto the prepared trays, allowing room for spreading. Bake for 10 minutes or until the tops feel firm. Leave the cookies on their trays for 2–3 minutes, then transfer to a wire rack to cool completely.

Chocolate brioche bread and butter pudding

Preparation time:	**SERVES 6**
20 mins	600 ml (21 fl oz) cream
	6 egg yolks
Cooking time:	75 g (1/3 cup) sugar
30 mins	200 g (7 oz) dark chocolate, roughly chopped
	1 brioche loaf, crusts removed, cut into cubes
	extra 200 g (7 oz) dark chocolate, roughly chopped
	sifted cocoa, for dusting

1   Preheat the oven to 180°C (350°F/Gas 4). Pour the cream into a heavy-based pan and simmer for 2–3 minutes. Put the egg yolks and sugar in a bowl and whisk until thick and creamy. Gradually whisk in the hot cream. Add the chocolate and stir until the mixture is smooth and the chocolate has melted.

2   Add the brioche and stand for 5 minutes. Place the extra chocolate into the bowl and stir until well combined. Lightly grease a 1.5 litre (6 cup) ovenproof dish. Pour the mixture into the dish and sit in a baking pan. Pour enough hot water into the pan to come 3 cm (1 1/4 inches) up the sides of the dish.

3   Bake for 30–35 minutes. Remove from the oven and stand for 10 minutes. Dust with cocoa. Serve with vanilla ice cream or softly whipped cream.

Winter midweek dinner

Entertaining friends and family can sometimes feel a little overwhelming, particularly if you try to do it midweek. It can be handily managed, though, with a menu that brings together food that is easily obtained, prepared and cooked to produce a simple but elegant meal.

MENU

Pass around the little Zucchini and corn cakes with Chilli dipping sauce while you add the finishing touches to the salmon. The Watercress salad has a fresh peppery flavour and crisp texture that goes perfectly with the richness of Baked orange salmon with orange gremolata. Add a big bowl of Salted roast potatoes to round off the meal. Everyone will want seconds of the dessert, Pears baked with Turkish delight. Accompany it with a big scoop of Rosewater and pistachio ice cream and sprinkle rose petals on top.

Pick up a bunch of roses on the way home for a stunning, simple centrepiece.

Think ahead

If you have time the evening before, you can get ahead by preparing the oranges and storing them in a covered container in the fridge. Wash the watercress and remove the sprigs, then wrap them in a clean tea towel and keep them in the vegetable crisper until just before serving. The Rosewater and pistachio ice-cream can be made up to a week ahead or, if you prefer, you can serve a scoop of vanilla ice-cream with the pears, drizzle over a little rosewater and top with the chopped pistachios. The menu serves four as it is, but can be doubled for larger crowds or halved for an intimate meal. And of course you don't have to serve it midweek – this menu is perfect for a dinner party any night of the week

No-fuss entertaining

If you're hosting a casual get-together, don't worry about a formal setting for the table. Just put the knives and forks in a large glass or vase in the centre of the table and let your guests help themselves.

Zucchini and corn cakes

Preparation time:

10 mins

Cooking time:

15 mins

SERVES 4

4 eggs

310 g (10½ oz) can corn kernels, drained

2 zucchini (courgettes), grated

2 spring onions (scallions), chopped

60 g (½ cup) self-raising flour

salt and freshly ground black pepper

1 tablespoon olive oil

Chilli dipping sauce

125 g (½ cup) sweet chilli sauce

juice of 1 lemon

extra spring onion (scallion), chopped

1   Put the eggs in a bowl and beat with a whisk to combine. Add the corn, zucchini and spring onions. Add the flour, salt and pepper and stir gently to combine.

2   Heat the oil in a heavy-based, non-stick frypan. Drop in spoonfuls of the batter and cook until golden underneath and the top starts to set. Turn and cook the other side for 1–2 minutes.

3   Remove the cakes from the pan. Put on a plate, cover, and keep warm. Continue cooking all the mixture in this way.

4   To make the dipping sauce, combine the chilli sauce, lemon juice and spring onions in a small bowl. Serve the cakes with sauce.

Watercress salad

Preparation time:
10 mins

Cooking time:
nil

SERVES 4

500 g (1 bunch) watercress

handful roughly chopped walnuts

splash white-wine vinegar

splash olive oil

Wash the watercress and remove the sprigs. Pat the sprigs dry with a paper towel and place in a large bowl. Add the walnuts, splash with a little white-wine vinegar and olive oil and toss to combine.

Salted roast potatoes

Preparation time:
10 mins

Cooking time:
45 mins

SERVES 4

1 kg (2 lb 4 oz) baby chats (new potatoes)

olive oil

sea salt

Put the potatoes in a large pan, cover with cold water, bring to the boil and simmer until tender. Drain, and leave to cool. Put each potato on a flat surface and flatten with the heel of your hand. Put the potatoes in an ovenproof dish, spray or brush with olive oil and sprinkle with sea salt. Bake in a moderate 180°C (350°F/Gas 4) oven for 15–20 minutes.

Baked orange salmon with orange gremolata

Preparation time:

25 mins

Cooking time:

20 mins

SERVES 4

6 small to medium oranges

4 salmon fillets

125 ml (1/2 cup) white wine

a little virgin olive oil

1/2 teaspoon fennel seeds

1 teaspoon sea salt flakes

freshly ground black pepper

20 g (1/3 cup) finely chopped flat-leaf (Italian) parsley

2 cloves garlic, finely chopped

1 Preheat the oven to 180°C (350°F/Gas 4). Finely grate the zest of two of the oranges and set aside. Remove the zest and pith from all the oranges and cut into slices. Put the orange slices in a pile down the centre of an ovenproof dish.

2 Lay the salmon fillets on top of the oranges in a single layer. Pour over the wine and drizzle the fillets with a little olive oil. Put the fennel seeds, sea salt and some freshly ground pepper in a small bowl and stir to combine. Sprinkle on top of the salmon.

3 Cut a sheet of baking paper large enough to fully cover the oranges and salmon. Run the paper under cold water and squeeze out the excess. Cover the salmon and oranges with the wet paper, tucking in around the edges. Bake for 12–15 minutes.

4 Make an orange gremolata by combining the orange zest, parsley and garlic in a bowl. Sprinkle the gremolata on top of the salmon. Serve with Salted roast potatoes and Watercress salad (page 347).

Pears baked with Turkish delight

Preparation time:

10 mins

Cooking time:

30 mins

SERVES 4

3 beurre bosc pears

100 g (3½ oz) pink rosewater Turkish delight,
 roughly chopped

Preheat the oven to 180°C (350°F/Gas 4). Line a baking tray with baking paper. Cut the pears in half lengthways and remove the seeds. Put the pear halves on the prepared tray and fill the centres with pieces of Turkish delight. Bake for 25–30 minutes or until the pears are tender and the Turkish delight is melted. Allow to cool slightly. Serve with Rosewater and pistachio ice cream. Sprinkle with fresh rose petals.

Rosewater and pistachio ice cream

Preparation time:

10 mins

Cooking time:

nil

SERVES 4

1 litre (4 cups) good-quality vanilla ice cream

65 g (½ cup) pistachio kernels, roughly chopped

60 ml (¼ cup) rosewater

Scoop the ice cream into a bowl but keep its container. Let it soften, but not melt. Add the rosewater and nuts and stir to combine. Return the ice cream to its container and refreeze.

Glossary

bok choy (pak choi)   a member of the cabbage family with a slightly mustardy taste. It has fleshy white stems and dark green leaves. Separate the leaves and wash well before use.

bulb spring onion   an immature onion that, if left in the ground, would grow to full size. Depending on when it is picked, it has a small, white bulb of varying size and long green tops. Normally sold in bunches.

caramelize   to cook until sugars, which either exist naturally in the food or are added (for example in a marinade), become golden brown.

chargrill pan   a heavy metal pan with raised ridges in parallel lines which gives food cooked on it an unmistakable stripey appearance.

dice   to chop food into very small, even cubes. Use a very sharp knife to do this.

dry-fry   to cook spices in a dry frying pan until they smell fragrant. Keep a close eye on spices cooked in this way, as they can burn in a very short space of time.

fillet   the particular cut of meat (e.g. pork or lamb), commonly taken from the top half of an animal's leg, or a neat cut from the fleshy part of a fish.

grease   to lightly coat a tin or dish with oil or melted butter to prevent food from sticking.

heavy-based pan   usually has a copper lining in the base which allows for even and constant distribution of heat across the whole base of the pan.

knead   to mix a stiff dough by manipulating it by hand in order to make it smooth.

mace   the outer lace-like covering of nutmeg. It has a similar but more delicate flavour.

purée   food blended or processed to a pulp.

reduce   to boil or simmer liquid in an uncovered pan so that the liquid evaporates and the mixture becomes thicker and more concentrated in flavour.

rest   to allow meat to sit, covered, for a period of time after it has cooked before slicing it. This enables the muscle fibres to relax and so retain the juices when cut.

score   to make incisions with a knife (usually into fish or meat) in a crossed pattern, without cutting all the way through. This ensures even cooking through thicker sections of the food.

sea salt   salt produced by the evaporation of sea water. The crystals are large and often flaky.

semolina   can be bought in packets from most supermarkets. It is derived from wheat.

shred   to cut food into small, narrow strips, either by hand, or using a grater or food processor with a shredding disc. Cooked meat may be shredded by pulling it apart with forks or your fingers.

simmer   to cook liquid, or food in a liquid, over low heat, just below boiling point. The surface of the liquid should be moving, with a few small bubbles coming to the surface.

skim   to remove fat or scum that comes to the surface of a liquid.

spring onions (scallions)   these long, slender immature onions with leaves have a mild, delicate flavour and both the green tops and the small white part can be eaten raw or cooked.

strain   to remove solids from a liquid by pouring it through a sieve. The solids are discarded, unless otherwise specified.

syrup   a sweetened liquid which has been reduced by simmering to a thicker consistency.

tofu (beancurd)   comes in varying consistencies. It absorbs the flavours of the food it is cooked with.

zest   the coloured skin of citrus fruits, usually lemon, orange and lime. It is often grated and added to mixtures, but avoid the bitter white pith.

Index